KAISER PRIMARY CENTER

MAKING WORDS

Multilevel, Hands-On, Developmentally Appropriate Spelling and Phonics Activities

P9-BBV-830

by
Patricia M. Cunningham
and Dorothy P. Hall

illustrated by
Tom Heggie

Cover photo by Dennis Fraise

ISBN No. 0-86653-806-2

Printing No. 191817161514

Copyright © 1994, Good Apple

Good Apple
23740 Hawthorne Boulevard
Torrance, CA 90505-5927
A Division of
Frank Schaffer Publications, Inc.

The purchase of this book entitles the buyer to reproduce student activity pages for classroom use only. Any other use requires written permission from Good Apple.

All rights reserved. Printed in the United States of America.

4557 14273 6

DEDICATION

For Our Children–Michelle, Suzanne, and David

A special thanks to
Rosalyn Morgan, photographer,
and Tonya Campbell, teacher–
both '92 graduates of Wake Forest University's
Elementary Education Program–
and to the children at
Clemmons Elementary School, Winston-Salem, N. C.,
who starred in the photos

Copyright © 1994, Good Apple

G1498

TABLE OF CONTENTS

GUIDE TO WARM-UP LESSONS

(One Vowel)

scratch   c   a (at/car)   ar   art   ash.......................................9
    at art/tar car cart cars/scar star scat cash rash trash crash chart scratch

splash   s   sl   al   ap   ash   s (plural) 10
    Al pal/lap sap Sal has/ash sash lash pass pals/laps/slap slaps slash splash

spends   sp   ed   en   en 11
    Ed Ned/end/den pen pens dens/send sped spend spends

strength   t   et   est..12
    he she set get net nest rest test sent/tens tent then stern tenth strength

spring   r   p   in   ing..13
    in pin pig rig rip rips nips/spin/snip/pins ping sing ring rings spring

tricks   s   sk   st   i (it/sir)   it   ick..........................14
    is it kit sit sir stir sick Rick tick skit skirt stick trick tricks

sports   sp   ot   o (top/or)   s pairs (sort-sorts)....................15
    or top/pot rot port stop/pots/spot sort sorts stops/spots sport sports

strong   s   t   ot   ong   o (go/got/sort)...........................16
    so no go got rot not/ton son song sort/rots torn tons tong tongs snort strong

thumbs   b   ub   ut..17
    us bus/sub tub/but hut huts/shut stub/bust must much bush thumb thumbs

trunks   r   st   ut   un   s pairs (run/runs).........................18
    us nut rut run sun sunk runs ruts/rust tusk stun stunk trunk trunks

Copyright © 1994, Good Apple

G1498

LESSONS INDEX (IN ALPHABETICAL ORDER)

Copyright © 1994, Good Apple

G1498

Copyright © 1994, Good Apple

G1498

Copyright © 1994, Good Apple

G1498

Copyright © 1994, Good Apple

G1498

an pan pen pal/lap nap lay pay/yap play leap lean plan plane/panel apple apply playpen

so top/pot pots/post/spot/stop poke poet sock stock spoke/pokes poets socket pocket pockets

to at sat pat pot tot toe toes pots/post poet poets paste taste potato teapot teapots potatoes

pen pet net set sent rent rest pest/pets/step spent rents enter reset resent repent present

*A two-day lesson or pick and choose!
is in pin pen pie ice rip ripe rice nice spin/pins pens pine rise risen ripen price spice spine since spices prices prince princes princess

be me mop mob sob rob pro poem pole mole role rope robe probe morsel problem problems

us in ink/kin ski skip skin/sink spin mink pink punk pump spunk minus pumpkin pumpkins

is us up pup sup use/Sue sip pep pie pies pipe pups pipes puppies

Ed up us use/Sue she due dues/used push spud sped shed pushed

an in ink/kin can nag gun gunk gain nick king quick quack quaking quacking

as at sat rat/art rut ruts/rust rest quest squat quart quarts square quarter quarters

at as air art/rat sat bat bar tar sir stir star stair rabbi rabbit rabbits

an in kin ran nag rag rig rain rank rang ring king grin gain grain raking

in red rid die dine deer/reed need rein rind ride rider/drier diner reindeer

so to rot ore sore tore/rote rose root roots/roost store stores rooter rooster roosters

Copyright © 1994, Good Apple
G1498

sailboat   s   sl   b   bl   ab   at   it   ot   ail   oil
> ***A two-day lesson or pick and choose!***
> at as is it bit sit sat bat/tab lot lots/lost/slot slit/list slat/salt/last stab slab slob
> blot boat boil toil soil sail tail bail bait basal blast boast/boats bloat bloats sailboat

sandwich   s   h   ad   and   ish
> ad had sad saw/was has/ash and hand sand dash disc dish wish sandwich

Saturday   s   st   tr   at   ay   ust   y (try, rusty)
> ***A two-day lesson or pick and choose!***
> as at ad sad sat rat/art Ray say day dry try tray stay star/arts dart dust rust arty
> tardy rusty dusty/study stray astray sturdy Saturday

scared   s   c   sc   ar   are   ear   ed (ending)
> as sea sad are/ear car scar card care/race dear/read/dare cared/raced scare scared

searched   c   h   ch   ad   ear   s/es (plural)   ed (reached)
> hear-here (homophones) ***A two-day lesson or pick and choose!***
> as he her she sad had are/ear car cars card care ears dear hear here each ache arch
> rash reach erase chase cheer crash arches search reached crashed searched

seashell   s   sh   ell   s/es (plural)   see-sea, heel-heal (homophones)
> seashell (compound word)
> he she sea see sell seal/sale heal heel shell leash easel easels shells leashes seashell

shadow   s   sh   ad   ash
> do ho so as ad ads ash/has had sad was/saw who wash dash soda show shadow

skylab   ay   s (pairs)   y (sky-balky)
> Al as say lay lab ask sky sly slay/lays labs balk balks balky skylab

sleeping   p   s   sl   in   eep   ing   ing (ending)
> is in pin pig pigs ping sing spin seep peel sling sleep seeing seeping peeling
> sleeping

smallest   s   m   sm   at   et   all   ell
> as at mat sat set met let all mall sell tell smell small stall stale smells smallest

sniffing   s   sn   in   s (plural)   in-inn (homophones)
> is if in inn sin fin fig figs fins sing/sign inns sniff sniffing

spiders   s   p   sp   ip   ide
> is sip Sid sir rip pie dip drip ripe rise ride side pier pride spied spider spiders

squeaked   s   qu   squ   ue   ed (ending)   e (ee-ea)
> see-sea (homophones)
> as ask use Sue due sea see seek seed ease used eased asked quake quaked squeak
> squeaked

stairs   st   at   ir   s-pairs (sit-sits)
> is as at sat rat/art/tar air sir sit sits stir rats/star stars stirs stair stairs

starfish   st   ar   at   air
> at sat hat rat/tar far air hair fair fish star stir stair stars stairs starfish

Copyright © 1994, Good Apple   G1498

Copyright © 1994, Good Apple

G1498

Copyright © 1994, Good Apple

G1498

MAKING WORDS AND CONNECTIONS ACROSS THE CURRICULUM

To be effective, phonics and spelling instruction should be tied as closely to what children are reading and learning about as possible. In selecting the word that ends the lesson, we have included many words which teachers use as part of their themes or units. The word *Amelia* is a great follow-up when reading the Amelia Bedelia books. *Duckling* connects to the tale of the ugly duckling. Here are some of the other curriculum connections possible from the words in this book.

Seasons/Weather: winter clouds thunder

Sports: baseball fishing hunting throws

Water: beaches bathtubs sailboat seashell islands swamps

Animals: animals chickens elephant feathers goldfish kittens lizards panther parrots puppies quacking rabbits reindeer roosters spiders starfish tigers tracks turtles whiskers jumping

Food/Nutrition: apples cereals crackers muffins oatmeal dinner oranges peanuts potatoes pumpkins sandwich

Places/Geography: globes bridges islands mountain pebbles swamps valleys jungles country

Celebrations: candles balloons present cheering dances parades flowers surprise camera

Folktales/Fairy Tales: creature giants monster castles palace princess treasure

People: cowboys daughter doctor drivers farmers parents friends

Travel: engines vehicle tractors parking anywhere

Time: morning nights Saturday Thursday always

Science: magnets planets skylab shadow

Math: addition counted millions computer

Music: trumpets keyboard dances

Copyright © 1994, Good Apple

G1498

MAKING WORDS–THEORY AND RESEARCH

Making Words is an activity in which children are individually given some letters and use these letters to make words. During the fifteen-minute activity, children make approximately fifteen words, beginning with two-letter words and continuing with three-, four-, five-letter and bigger words until the final word is made. The final word (a six-, seven-, or eight-letter word) always includes all the letters they have that day, and children are usually eager to figure out what word can be made from all these letters. Making Words is an active, hands-on, manipulative activity in which children discover letter-sound relationships and learn how to look for patterns in words. They also learn that changing just one letter or even just the sequence of the letters changes the whole word (Cunningham & Cunningham, 1992).

For the first Making Words lessons, we give the children only one vowel letter, but a different one for each lesson. The vowel letter is always written in red, and the children know they have to use it for every word. In these beginning lessons, the emphasis is on how words change as different letters are added and on helping children begin to understand the importance of where letters occur in the words. Once children have had some practice making words with just one vowel, we teach lessons which have two or more vowels. In these lessons we contrast the sound of the vowels by the order in which we have students make words. After children make the word *ball*, for example, we have them just change the vowel to make the word *bell*. After making the words, the children help the teacher to sort the words for patterns. They pull out all the words that begin alike or that have a particular spelling pattern or vowel sound. They also sort for endings (s, ed, ing), homophones (sea, see), and compound words.

Making Words is a multilevel, developmental activity because, within one instructional format, there are endless possibilities for discovering how our alphabetic system works. It is a quick, every-pupil response, manipulative activity with which children get actively involved. By beginning every Making Words activity with some short, easy words and ending with a big word that uses all the letters, the lessons provide practice for the slowest learners and challenge for all. Children who lack phonemic awareness seem to develop that awareness as they listen for the sounds in words in order to make them. Children who have phonemic awareness learn letter-sound correspondences and spelling patterns. Most importantly, children learn that there are patterns to be found in the way words are pronounced and spelled.

Spelling pattern and word family instruction has a long history in American reading instruction. Currently, research is converging from several areas which support the long-standing practice of word family/phonogram/spelling pattern instruction. The research of Treiman (1985) suggests that both children and adults find it much easier to divide syllables into their onsets (all letters before vowel) and rimes (vowel and what follows) than into any other units. Thus *Sam* is more easily divided into *S-am* than into *Sa-m* or *S-a-m*. It is easier and quicker for people to change *Sam* to *ham* and *jam* than it is to change *Sam* to *sat* and *sad*. In fact, Treiman concludes that the division of words into onset and rime is a "psychological reality." Wylie and Durrell (1970) listed thirty-seven phonograms which could be found in almost five hundred primary grade words. These high-utility phonograms are:

  ack, ail, ain, ake, ale, ame, an, ank, ap, ash, at, ate, aw, ay, eat, ell, est, ice, ick,
   ide, ight, ill, in, ine, ing, ink, ip, it, ock, oke, op, ore, ot, uck, ug, ump, unk.

Another area of research supporting spelling patterns is the research conducted on decoding by analogy (Goswami & Bryant, 1990). This research suggests that once children have some words which they can read and spell, they use these known words to figure out unknown words. A reader confronting the infrequent word *flounce* for the first time might access the known words *ounce* and *pounce* and then use these words to generate a probable pronunciation for *flounce*.

Copyright © 1994, Good Apple

1

Brain research provides a different sort of support for word family instruction. Current theory suggests that the brain is a pattern detector, not a rule applier, and that decoding a word occurs when the brain recognizes a familiar spelling pattern or, if the pattern itself is not familiar, searches through its store of words with similar patterns (Adams, 1990). To decode the unfamiliar word *knob*, for example, the child who knew many words that began with *kn* would immediately assign to the *kn* the "n" sound. The initial *kn* would be stored in the brain as a spelling pattern. If the child knew only a few other words with *kn* and hadn't read these words very often, that child would probably not have *kn* as a known spelling pattern and thus would have to do a quick search for known words which began with *kn*. If the child found the words *know* and *knew* and then tried this same sound on the unknown word *knob*, that child would have used the analogy strategy. Likewise, the child might know the pronunciation for *ob* because of having correctly read so many words containing the *ob* spelling pattern or might have had to access some words with *ob* to use them to come up with the pronunciation. The child who had no stored spelling patterns for *kn* or *ob* and no known words to access and compare to would be unlikely to successfully pronounce the unknown word *knob*.

The understanding that the brain is a pattern detector explains a great deal about the popularity of word family/phonogram/spelling pattern instruction since, in one-syllable words, the vowel and following letters is the pattern which is most helpful in decoding. Realizing that the brain functions as a pattern detector also explains why successful reading does not require that all the patterns be taught. The patterns exist in the words, and children who know that the patterns exist and who read widely will discover the patterns. Henderson (1990) suggests that word sorting is a powerful activity for developing children's spelling abilities.

If you ask the children what they think of Making Words, they will probably answer, "It's fun!" From the moment they get their letters, they begin moving them around and making whatever words they can. They are particularly eager to figure out the word that can be made with all the letters. Once the children begin making the words the teacher asks them to make, the activity is fast-paced and keeps the children involved. They also enjoy the sorting. Finding words that rhyme, words that begin alike, words which can all be changed into other words by just moving around the letters, and other patterns is like solving a riddle or a puzzle.

REFERENCES

Adams, M. J. *Beginning to Read: Thinking and Learning About Print.* Cambridge, MA: MIT Press, 1990.

Cunningham, P. M. *Phonics They Use: Words for Reading and Writing.* New York: HarperCollins, 1991.

Cunningham, P. M. and J. W. Cunningham. "Making Words: Enhancing the Invented Spelling-Decoding Connection." *The Reading Teacher,* 46, 106-115, 1992.

Goswami, U. and P. Bryant. *Phonological Skills and Learning to Read.* East Sussex, U.K.: Erlbaum Associates, 1990.

Henderson, E. H. *Teaching Spelling* (2nd ed.). Boston: Houghton Mifflin, 1990.

Trieman, R. "Onsets and Rimes as Units of Spoken Syllables: Evidence from Children." *Journal of Experimental Child Psychology,* 39, 161-181, 1985.

Wylie, R. E. and D. D. Durrell. "Teaching Vowels Through Phongrams." *Elementary English,* 47, 787-791, 1970.

Copyright © 1994, Good Apple

G1498

PREPARING AND TEACHING A MAKING-WORDS LESSON

Picture 1: The teacher has decided that *spider* is the word that will end the lesson. She has pulled out the large letter cards for *spider* and the zip-top bags with the small letter cards. Here she is brainstorming lots of little words that can be made from the letters in *spider*.

Picture 2: The teacher has decided which of the many small words that could be made will best illustrate some spelling patterns. She writes these words on large index cards.

Picture 3: She puts the large index cards on which she has written the words in a small brown envelope. On the outside of the envelope, she writes the words in the order the children will make them and the patterns she will have them sort for.

Picture 4: Each child chosen passes out one letter. When the lesson is over, the same child picks up this letter and returns it to the bag.

Photos by Rosalyn D. Morgan

Copyright © 1994, Good Apple

3

G1498

Picture 5: The teacher holds up and names each letter. The children hold up and name the matching letters on their cards. Both the large and small letter cards have the uppercase letter on one side and the lowercase letter on the other side. The consonant letters are written in black and the vowel letters are in red.

Picture 6: The children and teacher are ready to begin making words. Each child has the letters *i, e, d, p, r,* and *s.* These same letters are displayed on large cards in the pocket chart.

Picture 7: The teacher writes the numeral 2 on the board and says, "The two-letter word I want you to make today is *Ed.* I have a cousin whose name is Ed." She watches as the children quickly put the letters *E* and *d* in their holders and is glad to see most children displaying the uppercase *E.* After everyone makes the word *Ed* with the small letter cards, one child who made it correctly comes up and makes *Ed* with the large letter cards.

Picture 8: The children continue making three- and four-letter words. Now, they are going to make a five-letter word. The teacher tells them that they will make a five-letter word and asks them to hold up five fingers and to be sure to use that many letters. The teacher asks them to use five letters to make the word *pride.*

Photos by Rosalyn D. Morgan

Copyright © 1994, Good Apple

4

Picture 9: After everyone makes *pride* with small letters, a child who has made it correctly comes up and makes the word *pride* with the large letter cards.

Picture 10: The children know each lesson ends with a word that uses all their letters, and they always like to figure out what that word is. Today, however, the children are stumped. The teacher tells them to take all six letters and make an arachnid they are going to read about in science—*spider*! Here are all the words made in the lesson in the order in which they were made.

Picture 11: To conclude the lesson and draw children's attention to patterns, the teacher asks them to look at the words in the pocket chart. She picks up *Ed* and asks, "Who can come up here and hand me a word that rhymes with *Ed*?" A child hands her the word *red*. She then has someone find the two words that rhyme with *side—ride* and *pride*. Next, she has them find the three words that end in *s*: *pies*, *dies*, and *drips*. The teacher reminds the children that words having the same spelling pattern usually rhyme and asks, "What if I wanted to spell *fed*; what words that you have made today rhyme with *fed*?" The children decide that *fed* rhymes with *Ed* and *red* and would probably be spelled *f-e-d*. They also decide that *slide* rhymes with *side*, *ride*, and *pride* and would probably be spelled *s-l-i-d-e*.

Photos by Rosalyn D. Morgan

Copyright © 1994, Good Apple

G1498

HOW TO USE THIS BOOK

The Making-Words lessons in this book have been used by many primary teachers. Teachers pick, choose, and adapt the lessons to suit the needs of their own classes. Most teachers teach several warm-up lessons which contain only one vowel to help children meet immediate success and learn how to manipulate the letters to make words. Once children understand how to make words, the lessons usually contain two vowels. Eventually, we do not limit the number of vowels. This book contains ten warm-up lessons, but not all classes need to do that many.

Once you get past the warm-up lessons, choose (or create) lessons with words which can be integrated with your curriculum or which teach letter-sound patterns you want children to focus on. The lessons are ordered alphabetically by the big word that ends the lesson but can be done in any order. The index at the back indicates which letter patterns are sorted for in each lesson. Some teachers teach several lessons in a row which have a particular pattern children need to practice.

Each Making-Words lesson is multilevel in two ways. The children begin by making some very simple, short words and then make more complex, long words. The sorting is also multilevel in that children sort for consonants, blends, digraphs as well as phonograms, endings, compound words, and homophones. Since most primary classrooms contain children at all different stages of spelling/decoding ability, making easier and more difficult words and sorting for easier and more difficult patterns allow all children to increase their word knowledge. Asking children to spell two or three words based on the patterns sorted for increases the possibility that children will transfer their knowledge to real reading and writing.

Most lessons can be done in fifteen to twenty minutes, with approximately two-thirds of the time spent making words and the other one-third spent sorting and spelling. Some lessons are so rich in possibilities for word making and pattern sorting that they are specified as two-day lessons. If the lesson seems too long, you may omit certain words and/or patterns. With these longer lessons, many teachers like to make all the words on one day and then sort all the words the following day.

In teaching the lessons, you may want to omit certain words and add others. You may not want to sort for all the patterns or to sort for patterns not suggested. But, to keep the lesson multilevel, you will want to include words and patterns on a variety of levels. Some teachers worry that the least able children will not be able to make the long words and that the advanced children do not need to make the short words. Observations of these lessons indicate that if they are fast-paced, most children stay involved. Even if a child does not get every letter of a big word in place before another child makes that word with the big letters, the slower child usually gets some of the letters and then makes the word by matching to the model. Advanced children enjoy making the short words and are eager to figure out what word can be made with all the letters.

In addition to the lessons and the index, this book contains reproducible letter cards. Most teachers duplicate the letter pages on stiff paper (or index cards) using one color for the vowels and a different color for the consonants. The letter cards are then cut and stored in zip-top bags, and the letters needed are given out and taken up for each lesson. Many teachers also distribute simple folders made by cutting a file folder in half and then folding and stapling the bottom inch (see the pictures).

Copyright © 1994, Good Apple

6

G1498

Some teachers make take-home strips of the letters used in the lesson. The children can't wait to take the strips home and say, "I bet you don't know what word these letters will make!" The teacher encourages them to cut or tear the strip into letters once they get home and to show someone all the different words they can remember making and then show how they sorted them for patterns.

Making Words is a manipulative, developmental, multilevel activity which teachers and children enjoy. More importantly, children explore words and discover patterns, increase their word knowledge, and become better readers and writers.

PLANNING YOUR OWN MAKING-WORDS LESSONS

Once you get started making words, you will find that many of the words which tie into your content are not included in our lessons. It is fun and easy to plan lessons of your own. Here are the steps we went through to plan our lessons.

1. Decide what the final word in the lesson will be. In choosing this word, consider its number of vowels, child interest, what curriculum tie-ins you can make, and what letter-sound patterns you can draw children's attention to through the word sorting at the end.
2. Make a list of shorter words that can be made from the letters of the final word.
3. From all the words you listed, pick approximately fifteen words that include:
   a. Words that you can sort for the pattern(s) you want to emphasize.
   b. Little words and big words so that the lesson is a multilevel lesson.
   c. Words that can be made with the same letters in different places (barn/bran) so children are reminded that when spelling words, the order of the letters is crucial.
   d. A proper name or two to remind them where we use capital letters.
   e. Words that most of the students have in their listening vocabularies.
4. Write all the words on index cards and order them from smallest to biggest.
5. Once you have the two-letter, three-letter, etc., words together, order them further so that you can emphasize letter patterns and how changing the position of the letters or changing or adding just one letter results in a different word.
6. Store the cards in an envelope. Write on the envelope the words in order and the patterns you will sort for at the end.

Copyright © 1994, Good Apple

G1498

STEPS IN TEACHING A MAKING-WORDS LESSON

1. Place the large letter cards needed for this lesson in a pocket chart or along the chalk ledge.

2. Have designated children give one letter to each child. (Let the passer keep the zip-top bag containing that letter and have the same child collect the letters when the lesson is over. Give out only letters needed for the lesson.)

3. Hold up and name the letters on the large letter cards and have the children hold up and name their matching small letter cards.

4. Write the numeral 2 (or 3, if there are no two-letter words in this lesson) on the board. Tell students to take two letters and make the first word. Say the word and use the word in a sentence if necessary.

5. Have the children make the word using their small letter cards.

6. Have a child who has made the word correctly make the same word with the large letter cards. Encourage anyone who did not make the word correctly to fix his or her word when it has been shown made correctly.

7. Continue having students make words, erasing and changing the number on the board to indicate the number of letters needed. Use the words in simple sentences if necessary to access meaning. Remember to cue students as to whether they are just changing one letter, changing letters around or taking all their letters out to make a word from scratch. Cue them when the word you want them to make is a name, and send a child who has started that name with a capital letter to make the word with the big letters.

8. Before telling them the last word ask, "Has anyone figured out what word we can make with all our letters?" If so, congratulate those children, have them make the word with their small letter cards, and have one of them make it with the big letters. If not, say something like, "I love it when I can stump you. Use all your letters and make _____."

   (Some teachers make the words on one day and then do steps nine and ten the following day.)

9. Once all the words have been made, take the index cards on which you have written the words and place them one at a time (in the same order children made them) along the chalk ledge or in the pocket chart. Have children say and spell the words with you as you do this. Use these words for sorting and pointing out patterns. Pick a word, point out a particular spelling pattern, and ask children to find the others with that same pattern. Line these words up so that the pattern is visible.

10. To get maximum transfer to reading and writing, have students use the patterns they have sorted to spell a few new words that you say.

WARM-UP LESSON #1

(The children have the vowel letter *a* and the consonant letters *c, c, h, r, s,* and *t.*)

MAKE WORDS

Take two letters and make *at*.
Add a letter to make the three-letter word *art*.
Change the letters around and turn *art* into *tar*.
Now change just one first letter and *tar* can become *car*.
Now we are going to make some four-letter words. Hold up four fingers! Add one letter to *car* and you have *cart*. (The little boy pushed his cart.)
Change the last letter and you can change *cart* into *cars*. Instead of one cart you now have a number of cars.
Don't take any letters out, change the letters around, and you can make *cars* into *scar*.
Change one letter and you can change *scar* into *star*. (Maybe someday you will be a star.)
Now take all the letters out and make another four-letter word, *scat*. (The woman told the cat to scat.)
Let's make another word, *cash*.
Change just the first letter and you can change *cash* into *rash*. (When you have poison ivy, you have a rash.)
Now let's make a five-letter word. Hold up five fingers! Add a letter to *rash* and you can make *trash*.
Change the first letter and you can change your *trash* to *crash*. (Often race-car drivers end up in a crash.)
Let's make another five-letter word. Use five letters to make *chart*. (The teacher likes to make a new chart every time we study something new.)
Has anyone figured out what word we can make with all seven letters? Take all seven of your letters and make *scratch*.

SORT

When the children have made *scratch*, draw their attention to the words they made and help them sort for a variety of patterns: *at, art, tar, car, cart, cars, scar, star, scat, cash, rash, trash, crash, chart, scratch*.
Take the word *car* and have them find the other words that begin with *c–cart, cars, cash*.
Take the word *car* and have them find the other *a-r* words–*scar* and *star*.
Take the word *art* and have them find the other *a-r-t* words–*cart, chart*.
Take the word *cash* and have them find the other *a-s-h* words–*rash, crash,* and *trash*.
Take the word *at* and have the children find words that have the same vowel sound as in *at–cash, scat, rash, trash, crash,* and *scratch*.
Take the word *car* and have the children find words that have the same vowel sound as in *car–art, tar, cart, cars, scar, star,* and *chart*.

WRITING AND NEED TO SPELL

What if you were writing about yourself and you needed to spell *smart*? Which words would help you spell *smart*? What if you were writing about swimming and needed to spell *splash*?

Copyright © 1994, Good Apple

WARM-UP LESSON # 2

(The children have the vowel letter *a* and the consonant letters *h, l, p, s,* and *s.*)

MAKE WORDS

Take two letters and make *Al.*

Now add a letter to make the three-letter word *pal.*

Now this is a real trick. Don't add any letters and don't take any away. Just change where some of the letters are and you can change *pal* to *lap.*

Change just the first letter and you can change *lap* into *sap.* (The sap runs in some trees in the early spring.)

Now change the last letter and you can make the name *Sal.* (Remember to change the *s* to the uppercase *S* for a name.)

Now make the three-letter word *has.* (This has to be an easy word to make.)

Don't add any letters and don't take any away. Just change where some of the letters are and you can change *has* into *ash.* (There is an ash tree in our backyard.)

Add a letter to *ash* and you can make the word *sash.* (Her dress had a sash around the waist.)

Now change just the first letter and you can make *lash* (like an eyelash).

Now let's make another four-letter word. Make the word *pass.* (The boy can pass the football quickly.)

Change just one letter and you can make *pals.*

Now this is a real trick. Don't add any letters and don't take any away. Just change where some of the letters are and you can change *pals* to *laps.* (The swimmers will swim two laps for this race.)

Believe it or not, you can make another word with these same four letters. Move your letters around and change *laps* to *slap.*

Now let's make some five-letter words. Hold up five fingers! Just add one letter to make the five-letter word *slaps.*

Now take the letters out and start over again to make the next word, *slash.* (Watch out with the knife so that you don't slash someone.)

Has anyone figured out what word we can make with all six letters? Take all six of your letters and make *splash.*

SORT

When the children have made *splash,* draw their attention to the words they made and help them sort for a variety of patterns: *Al, pal, lap, sap, Sal, has, ash, sash, lash, pass, pals, laps, slap, slaps, slash, splash.*

Take the word *sap* and have them find the other words that begin with *s* (*Sal, sash*).

Take the word *slap* and have them find the other words that begin with *sl* (*slaps, slash*).

Take the word *Al* and have them find the other words that have *al* in them (*pal, Sal, pals*).

Take the word *lap* and have them find other words with *ap* in them (*sap, slap, slaps*).

Take the word *ash* and have them find the other words that have *ash* in them (*sash, lash, slash, splash*).

Take the word *pals* and have them find the other plural words (*laps, slaps*).

WRITING AND NEED TO SPELL

What if you were writing about night noises and needed to spell *snap*? Which words would help you spell *snap*? What if you wanted to write *crash*? Which words would help you to spell *crash*?

Copyright © 1994, Good Apple

G1498

WARM-UP LESSON #3

(The children have the vowel letter *e* and the consonant letters *d, n, p, s,* and *s.*)

MAKE WORDS

Take two letters and make *Ed*. My uncle's name is Ed. Remember to use the uppercase *E* when beginning to make a name.

Add a letter to *Ed* to make the three-letter word *Ned*. (Ned needs a capital letter for his name also.)

Just change the letters around and you can change *Ned* into the new word *end*. (This is not the end of the lesson.)

Now change them around again and make the word *den*.

Let's make one more three-letter word. Change the first letter and you have *pen*.

Now let's make a four-letter word. Hold up four fingers! Add a letter to *pen* and you can make the plural *pens*. (I have pens in many colors.)

Change the first letter and you can change *pens* to *dens*.

Now this is a real trick. Don't add any letters and don't take any away. Just change where some of the letters are and you can change *dens* to *send*. (I will send you a letter.)

There is one more word we will make with four letters. Make the word *sped*. (He sped down the hill on his bike.)

Let's make a five-letter word. Use five letters to make *spend*.

Now, add one letter to the end of *spend* to make the six-letter word *spends*. (She spends all her allowance each week.)

SORT

When the children have made *spends*, draw their attention to the words they made and help them sort for a variety of patterns: *Ed, Ned, end, den, pen, pens, dens, send, sped, spend, spends.*

Take the word *sped* and have them find the other words that begin with *sp* (*spend, spends*).

Take the word *Ed* and have them find the other *ed* word (*Ned*).

Take the word *den* and have them find the other *en* words (*pen, pens, den, dens*).

Take the word *send* and have them find the other *end* words (*spend, spends*).

WRITING AND NEED TO SPELL

What if you were writing about snow and needed to spell *sled*? Which words would help you spell *sled*? What if you wanted to spell *men*? Which words would help you spell *men*?

Copyright © 1994, Good Apple

WARM-UP LESSON #4

(The children have the vowel letter *e* and the consonant letters *g, h, n, r, s, t,* and *t.*)

MAKE WORDS

Take two letters and make *he.*
Now take three letters and make the three-letter word *she.*
Now use three letters and make the word *set.* (Set the table if you want to help with dinner.)
Change the first letter in *set* and you can make the word *get.*
Change the first letter again and you can make *net.* (You can catch a fish in the net.)
Add one letter to *net* and you can make *nest.* (The bird built a nest outside my window in a tree.)
Change just the first letter in *nest* and you can make *rest.*
Change the first letter again and you can make the word *test.*
Now we will make another four-letter word, *sent.* (Dad sent me to the store.)
Don't add any letters and don't take any away. Just change where some of the letters are and you can change *sent* into *tens.* (I can count by tens.)
Just change the last letter in the word *tens* and you can make *tent.*
The last four-letter word we are going to make is *then.*
Next we are going to make a five-letter word. Hold up five fingers! Use five letters to make the word *stern.* (The teacher had a stern look on her face!)
Another five-letter word is *tenth.* (She was the tenth one in line.)
Has anyone figured out what word we can make with all eight letters? Take all eight of your letters and make *strength.* (He has the strength to lift almost anything.)

SORT

When the children have made *strength,* draw their attention to the words they made and help them sort for a variety of patterns: *he, she, set, get, net, nest, rest, test, sent, tens, tent, then, stern, tenth, strength.*
Take the word *test* and have them find the other words that begin with *t* (*tens, tent, tenth*).
Take the word *set* and have them find the other words that have *et* in them (*get, net*).
Take the word *nest* and have them find other words with *est* in them (*rest, test*).

WRITING AND NEED TO SPELL

What if you were writing about your pet and needed to spell *vet*? Which words would help you spell *vet*? What if you wanted to write *pest*? Which words would help you to spell *pest*?

Copyright © 1994, Good Apple

G1498

WARM-UP LESSON #5

(The children have the vowel letter *i* and the consonant letters *g, n, p, r,* and *s.*)

MAKE WORDS

Take two letters and make *in.*
Add a letter to make the three-letter word *pin.*
Change just one letter and turn your *pin* into *pig.*
Now change just one letter and your *pig* can become *rig.* (Sometimes we call a big truck a rig.)
Let's make one more three-letter word, *rip.*
Now let's make a four-letter word. Hold up four fingers! Add a letter to *rip* and you can make *rips.*
Change the first letter and you can change your *rips* to *nips.* (Sometimes a very young puppy nips at your feet.)
Now this is a real trick. Don't add any letters and don't take any away. Just change where some of the letters are and you can change *nips* to *spin.*
Believe it or not, you can make another word with these same four letters. Move your letters around and change *spin* to *snip.* (When we make a small cut, we say we snip it off.)
There is one more word which you can make with these same four letters. Move your letters around one more time and change *snip* to *pins.* (He found two safety pins.)
Let's make two more four-letter words. Use four letters to make *sing.*
Now change just the first letter and make *ring.*
Now we will make a five-letter word. Add a letter to change *ring* to *rings.*
Has anyone figured out what word we can make with all six letters? Take all six of your letters and make *spring.*

SORT

When the children have made *spring,* draw their attention to the words they made and help them sort for a variety of patterns: *in, pin, pig, rig, rip, rips, nips, spin, snip, pins, sing, ring, rings, spring.*
Take the word *rig* and have them find the other words that begin with *r* (*rip, rips, ring, rings*).
Take the word *pin* and have them find the other words that begin with *p* (*pig, pins*).
Take the word *in* and have them find the other *in* words (*pin, spin*).
Take the word *ring* and have them find the other *ing* words (*sing, rings, spring*).

WRITING AND NEED TO SPELL

What if you were writing about fish and needed to spell *fin*? Which words would help you spell *fin*? What if you were writing about birds and needed to spell *wing*?

Copyright © 1994, Good Apple G1498

WARM-UP LESSON #6

(The children have the vowel letter *i* and the consonant letters *c, k, r, s,* and *t.*)

MAKE WORDS

Take two letters and make *is.*
Now, change one letter to make the word *it.*
Just add one letter and you can make the three-letter word *kit.* (I play hospital with my doctor's kit.)
Change just the first letter and you can change *kit* to *sit.*
Change just the last letter and you can change *sit* into *sir.*
Now add one letter and you can make the four-letter word *stir.* (Stir the paints before you begin to paint your picture.)
Let's make another four-letter word, *sick.* (I don't like to be sick.)
Change the first letter and make the name *Rick.* Remember to use an uppercase letter to begin the name.
Change just the first letter and you can make the word *tick.*
Take all the letters out and make the four-letter word *skit.* (I have a part in the skit our class will put on.)
Let's make some five-letter words. Hold up five fingers! Just add one letter to change the four-letter word *skit* into the five-letter word *skirt.*
Now make the five-letter word *stick.*
Change the first two letters and you can make the word *trick.*
Has anyone figured out what word we can make with all six letters? Take all six of your letters and make *tricks.*

SORT

When the children have made *tricks,* draw their attention to the words they made and help them sort for a variety of patterns: *is, it, kit, sit, sir, stir, sick, Rick, tick, skit, skirt, stick, trick, tricks.*
Take the word *sit* and have them find the other words that begin with *s* (*sir, sick*).
Take the word *skit* and have them find the other word that begins with *sk* (*skirt*).
Take the word *stir* and have them find the other word that begins with *st* (*stick*).
Take the word *it* and have them find the other words that have *it* in them (*kit, sit, skit*).
Take the word *sick* and have them find other words with *ick* in them (*Rick, tick, stick, trick, tricks*).
Take the word *it* and have them find the other words that have the same vowel sound in them (*is, kit, sit, sick, Rick, tick, skit, stick, trick, tricks*).
Take the word *sir* and have them find other words with the same vowel sound (*sir, stir, skirt*).

WRITING AND NEED TO SPELL

What if you were writing about animals and needed to spell *bit*? Which words would help you spell *bit*? What if you wanted to write *kick*? Which words would help you to spell *kick*?

WARM-UP LESSON #7

(The children have the vowel letter *o* and the consonant letters *p, r, s, s,* and *t.*)

MAKE WORDS

Take two letters and make *or*.

Now make the three-letter word *top*.

Now this is a real trick. Don't add any letters and don't take any away. Just change where some of the letters are and you can change *top* to *pot*.

Change just the first letter and you can change *pot* into *rot*. *(Sometimes my bananas rot while sitting on the shelf.)*

Now let's make a four-letter word. Hold up four fingers! Use one more letter and you can make *port*. (Ships come into a port to let off cargo.)

Now here is a four-letter word you all know how to make, *stop*.

Now this is a real trick. Don't add any letters and don't take any away. Just change where some of the letters are and you can change *stop* to *pots*.

Believe it or not, you can make another word with these same four letters. Move your letters around and change *pots* to *spot*. (I got a spot on my shirt while eating blueberry pie.)

Let's make another four-letter word. Use four letters to make *sort*.

Now just add one letter and make the next word *sorts*.

Now we will make another five-letter word. Make the word *stops*.

Now don't add any letters and don't take any away. Just change where some of the letters are and change *stops* to *spots*.

We will make another five-letter word. Make the word *sport*.

Has anyone figured out what word we can make with all six letters? Take all six of your letters and make *sports*.

SORT

When the children have made *sports*, draw their attention to the words they made and help them sort for a variety of patterns: *or, top, pot, rot, port, stop, pots, spot, sort, sorts, stops, spots, sport, sports*.

Take the word *spot* and have them find the other words that begin with *sp* (*spots, sport, sports*).

Take the word *pot* and have them find the other words that have *ot* in them (*rot, pots, spot, spots*).

Take the words *pot* and *pots* and have them find other s-pairs (*sort-sorts, stop-stops, spot-spots, sport-sports*).

Take the word *top* and have them find the other words that have the same vowel sound (*top, pot, rot, stop, pots, spot, stops, spots*).

Take the word *or* and have them find the other words that have the same vowel sound (*port, sort, sorts, sport, sports*).

WRITING AND NEED TO SPELL

What if you were writing about a horse and needed to spell *trot*? Which words would help you spell *trot*? What if you wanted to write *trots*? Which words would help you to spell *trots*?

Copyright © 1994. Good Apple

G1498

WARM-UP LESSON #8

(The children have the vowel letter *o* and the consonant letters *g, n, r, s,* and *t*.)

MAKE WORDS

Take two letters and make *so*.
Change just one letter and you can make the word *no*.
Change a letter again and change *no* into *go*.
Now we are going to make some three-letter words. Add a letter to *go* and make the three-letter word *got*.
Change just the first letter and you can change *got* into *rot*. (The tomatoes will rot if they are not picked soon.)
Now change the first letter and you can change *rot* into *not*.
Don't add any letters and don't take any away. Just change where some of the letters are and you can change *not* into *ton*. (The box felt like it weighed a ton.)
Change the first letter of *ton* and you can make *son*. (The father played ball with his son.)
Now let's make a four-letter word. Add a letter to *son* and make *song*.
Take the letters out and start all over to make the word *sort*. (We will sort words next!)
Don't add any letters and don't take any away. Just change where some of the letters are and you can change *sort* into *rots*.
The next four-letter word we are going to make is *torn*. (My old jeans are torn.)
Take the letters out and start all over to make the word *tons*.
Change just the last letter and you can make *tong*.
We are now going to make five-letter words. Hold up five fingers! Add one letter to *tong* and make the word *tongs*. (They often put tongs at the salad bar.)
The next five-letter word to make is *snort*.
Has anyone figured out what word we can make with all six letters? Take all six of your letters and make *strong*.

SORT

When the children have made *strong*, we draw their attention to the words they made and help them sort for a variety of patterns: *so, no, go, got, rot, not, ton, son, song, sort, rots, torn, tons, tong, tongs, snort, strong*.
Take the word *so* and have them find the other words that begin with *s* (*son, song, sort*).
Take the word *ton* and have them find the other words that begin with *t* (*torn, tons, tong, tongs*).
Take the word *got* and have them find the other words that have *ot* in them (*rot, not*).
Take the word *song* and have them find other words with *ong* in them (*tong, tongs, strong*).
Ask the children to find words with the same vowel sound as *go* (*no, so*).
Ask the children to find words with the same vowel sound as *got* (*rot, not, song, rots, tong, tongs, strong*).
Ask the children to find words with the same vowel as *sort* (*torn, snort*).

WRITING AND NEED TO SPELL

What if you were writing about your new garden and needed to spell *plot*? Which words would help you spell *plot*? What if you wanted to write *long*? Which words would help you to spell *long*?

Copyright © 1994. Good Apple

G1498

WARM-UP LESSON #9

(The Children have the vowel letter *u* and the consonant letters *b, h, m, c, s,* and *t.*)

MAKE WORDS

Take two letters and make *us.*

Now add a letter to make the three-letter word *bus.*

Now this is a real trick. Don't add any letters and don't take any away. Just change where some of the letters are and you can change *bus* to *sub.*

Change just the first letter and you can change *sub* into *tub.* (We take a bath in a tub.)

Don't add any letters and don't take any away. Just change where some of the letters are and you can change *tub* into *but.* (I wanted to go, but my mother said no.)

Change just the first letter and you can make the word *hut.* (We made a little hut in the woods.)

Now let's make a four-letter word. Hold up four fingers! Just add a letter to *hut* and you can make *huts.*

Believe it or not, you can make another word with these same four letters. Move your letters around and change *huts* to *shut.* (Please shut the door.)

Let's make some more four-letter words. Use four letters to make *stub.* (Be careful or you might stub your toe.)

Change the letters around and you can change *stub* into *bust.*

Now just change the first letter and make the next word *must.* (Mother said you must clean your room.)

The next four-letter word to make is *much.* (How much money do you have?)

The last four-letter word is *bush.* (The bush in my yard is full of berries.)

Now we will make a five-letter word. Make the word *thumb.*

Has anyone figured out what word we can make with all six letters? Yes, the plural of thumb is made by adding an *s* to *thumb.* Take all six of your letters and make *thumbs.*

SORT

When the children have made *thumbs,* draw their attention to the words they made and help them sort for a variety of patterns: *us, bus, sub, tub, but, hut, huts, shut, stub, bust, must, much, bush, thumb, thumbs.*

Take the word *bus* and have them find the other words that begin with *b (but, bust, bush).*

Take the word *sub* and have them find the other words that have *ub* in them *(tub, stub).*

Take the word *hut* and have them find other words with *ut* in them *(huts, shut).*

WRITING AND NEED TO SPELL

What if you were writing about bears and needed to spell *cub?* Which words would help you spell *cub?* What if you wanted to write *nut?* Which words would help you to spell *nut?*

Copyright © 1994. Good Apple

G1498

WARM-UP LESSON #10

(The children have the vowel letter *u* and the consonant letters *k, n, r, s,* and *t.*)

MAKE WORDS

Take two letters and make *us.*
Now take three letters and make the three-letter word *nut.*
Change just the first letter and you can change *nut* into *rut.* (Don't fall into the rut.)
Now change the last letter and you can change *rut* into *run.*
Change the first letter in *run* and you can make the word *sun.*
Add one letter to *sun* and you can make *sunk.* (The boat sunk.)
Take all your letters out and make another four-letter word, *runs.*
Change just one letter and make *ruts.*
Don't add any letters and don't take any away. Just change where some of the letters are and you can change *ruts* into *rust.* (The metal was beginning to rust.)
The next four-letter word we are going to make is *tusk.* (The elephant had lost a tusk.)
Now let's make the last four-letter word, *stun.* (His plan was to stun the teacher and make 100!)
Next we are going to make a five-letter word. Hold up five fingers! Add one letter to *stun* and make the word *stunk.* (The skunk stunk.)
Just change the first two letters and make the next word *trunk.* (My sister packed a trunk to take to college.)
Has anyone figured out what word we can make with all six letters? Yes, the plural of *trunk* is made by adding an *s* to *trunk.* Take all six of your letters and make *trunks.*

SORT

When the children have made *trunks,* we draw their attention to the words they made and help them sort for a variety of patterns: *us, nut, rut, run, sun, sunk, runs, ruts, rust, tusk, stun, stunk, trunk, trunks.*
Take the word *rut* and have them find the other words that begin with *r* (*run, runs, ruts, rust*).
Take the word *stun* and have them find the other word that begins with *st* (*stunk*).
Take the word *nut* and have them find the other words that have *ut* in them (*rut, ruts*).
Take the word *sun* and have them find other words with *un* in them (*run, runs, stun*).
Ask the children to find s-pairs like *run-runs, rut-ruts, trunk-trunks.*

WRITING AND NEED TO SPELL

What if you were writing about making a sandwich and needed to spell *cut?* Which words would help you spell *cut?* What if you wanted to write *bun?* Which words would help you to spell *bun?*

Copyright © 1994, Good Apple

G1498

LETTERS:  a i i o d d n t

WORDS TO MAKE:

Give children clues about how many letters to use and how many letters to change. "Now we're going to make some two-letter words. Hold up two fingers! Add one letter to the word *ad*, an advertisement, and have the three-letter word *add*. When you do your math you add numbers." Also alert the children when they should just change the vowel to make a new word. "Change the vowel in *dad* and you will have a new word, *did*." Remind the children, "When you have words like *and/Dan,* you only have to change the letters around to make the word *and* into the new word *Dan*." For the words *into*, *idiot*, and *addition*, have them take all the letters out to make the new word.

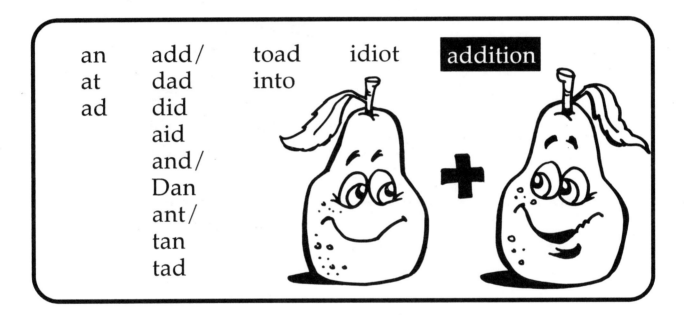

an	add/	toad	idiot	**addition**
at	dad	into		
ad	did			
	aid			
	and/			
	Dan			
	ant/			
	tan			
	tad			

SORT FOR: d   ad   an   into (compound word)
ad, add (homophones)

WRITING AND NEED TO SPELL:

glad (-ad)

plan (-an)

(Perhaps they are writing about a birthday party!)

Copyright © 1994, Good Apple

G1498

LETTERS:  a a l s w y

WORDS TO MAKE:

Give children clues about how many letters to use and how many letters to change. "Now we're going to make some three-letter words. Hold up three fingers! Change just the first letter and you can change the word *say* into *way*," or "Change just the last letter and you can change the word *lay* into *law*." Remind the children, "When you have words like *was/saw*, you only have to change the letters around to make the word *was* into the new word *saw*." For an unusual word like *slay*, give them a meaning they might understand. "The brave knight can slay the dragon with a thrust of his sword."

as	was/	laws/	always
	saw	slaw	
	say	sway	
	way	away	
	lay	slay/	
	law	lays	

SORT FOR: s   l   sl   ay   aw

WRITING AND NEED TO SPELL:

clay (-ay)

draw (-aw)

(Perhaps they are writing about an art project!)

Copyright © 1994, Good Apple

G1498

LETTERS:  a a e i l m

WORDS TO MAKE:

Give children clues about how many letters to use and how many letters to change. "Now we're going to make some four-letter words. Hold up four fingers! Change the vowel and you can change the word *lame* into *lime*." Remind the children, "When you have words like *lime/mile* you only have to change the letters around to make the word *lime* into the new word *mile*." Alert the children when they should take all the letters out and start from scratch to make a new word. "Now take all the letters out and start over and make the world *elm*." For an unusual word like *elm*, give them a meaning they might understand. "One tree that grows in this area is the elm tree." Also when there are homophones–*male*, *mail*–give the children the meanings as you ask them to make the words.

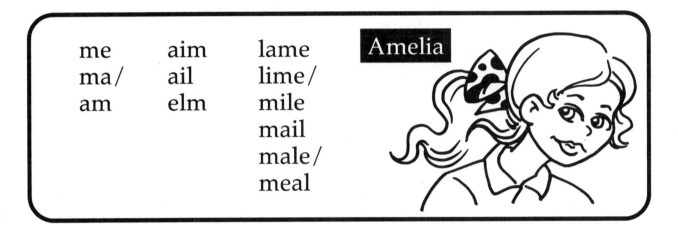

me	aim	lame
ma/	ail	lime/
am	elm	mile
		mail
		male/
		meal

Amelia

SORT FOR: m ail   mail, male (homophones)

WRITING AND NEED TO SPELL:

> pail (-ail)
>
> snail (-ail)

(Perhaps they are writing about the beach!)

Copyright © 1994, Good Apple

LETTERS:  a a i l m n s

WORDS TO MAKE:

Give children clues about how many letters to use and how many letters to change. "Now we're going to make some four-letter words. Hold up four fingers! Change just the first letter and you can change the word *mail* into *nail*." Also alert the children when they should take all the letters out and start from scratch to make a new word. "Now take all the letters out and start over and make the word *nasal*." For an unusual word like *nasal*, give them a meaning they might understand: "When our noses are stuffy, we say that we have nasal congestion."

an	Sam	main	snail/	salami
am	aim	mail	slain	animal
		nail	nasal	**animals**
		sail		
		slam		
		slim		

SORT FOR: s   sl   am   ail   ain

WRITING AND NEED TO SPELL:

trail (-ail)

jam (-am)

(Perhaps they are writing about being lost in the woods!)

LETTERS:  a e e h n r w y

WORDS TO MAKE:

Give children clues about how many letters to use and how many letters to change. "Now we're going to make some four-letter words. Hold up four fingers! Change just the first letter and you can change the word *hear* into *near*." Alert the children when they should take all the letters out and start from scratch to make a new word. "Now take all the letters out and start over and make the word *newer*." (Also when there are homophones–*here, hear*–in a lesson, give the children the meaning of the two words as you ask them to make the words.)

we	any	here	where	anywhere
an	are/	hear	newer	
	ear	near		
	her	wear		
		were		
		when		

SORT FOR: w h wh ear (Point out both sounds.)
here, hear (homophones)
anywhere (compound word)

WRITING AND NEED TO SPELL:

fear (-ear)

spear (-ear)

(Perhaps they are writing about a jungle dream!)

LETTERS:  a e l p p s

WORDS TO MAKE:

Give children clues about how many letters to use and how many letters to change. "Now we're going to make some three-letter words. Hold up three fingers! Change just the first letter and you can change the world *lap* into *sap*." Remind the children, "When you have words like *pal/lap*, you only have to change the letters around to make the word *pal* into the new word *lap*." For an unusual word like *lapse*, give them a meaning they might understand. "The teacher had a lapse in memory and could not remember the new boy's name."

as	pal/	slap/	pleas/	apples
Al	lap	pals	lapse	
	sap	apes/	apple	
	ape/	peas		
	pea			
	sea			
	spa			

SORT FOR: p   ap   s (plural)

WRITING AND NEED TO SPELL:

　　　　trap (-ap)

　　　　traps (-s)

(Perhaps they are writing about hunting or fishing!)

LETTERS:  a e e l p s

WORDS TO MAKE:

Give children clues about how many letters to use and how many letters to change. "Now we're going to make some four-letter words. Hold up four fingers! Change just the first letter and you can change the word *peal* into *seal*." Remind the children, "When you have words like *seal/sale* you only have to change the letters around to make the word *seal* into *sale*." For an unusual word like *asp*, give them a meaning they might understand. "An asp is a small, poisonous snake found in Africa and Europe." Also, remember to give the children meanings for the two pairs of homophones–*see, sea* and *peel, peal*–when asking them to make those words.

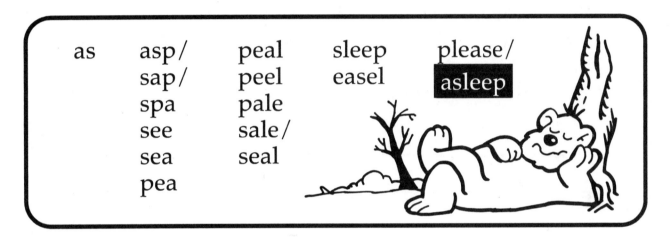

as	asp/	peal	sleep	please/
	sap/	peel	easel	asleep
	spa	pale		
	see	sale/		
	sea	seal		
	pea			

SORT FOR: s p ea eal ale
see, sea; peel, peal (homophones)

WRITING AND NEED TO SPELL:
squeal (-eal)

whale (-ale)

(Perhaps they are writing about a trip to the aquarium!)

LETTERS:  a o o b l l n s

WORDS TO MAKE:

Give children clues about how many letters to use and how many letters to change. "Now we're going to make some four-letter words. Hold up four fingers! Change just the first letter and you can change the word *soon* into *loon*." Remind the children, "When you have words like *ban/nab* you only have to change the letters around to make the word *ban* into the word *nab*." For an unusual word like *nab*, give them a meaning they might understand. "I hope the police will nab the thief today!"

on	ban/	ball	loans/	balloon
an	nab	also	salon	balloons
	lab	soon		
	all	loon		
		loan		

SORT FOR: b l ab oon

WRITING AND NEED TO SPELL:

crab (-ab)

moon (-oon)

(Perhaps they are writing about a fisherman!)

Copyright © 1994, Good Apple

G1498

LETTERS:  *aaebbllls*

WORDS TO MAKE:

Give children clues about how many letters to use and how many letters to change. "Now we're going to make some four-letter words. Hold up four fingers! Change just the vowel and you can change the word *ball* into *bell*. Change just the first letter of *bell* and you have a new word, *sell*." Remind the children, "When you have words like *seal/sale* you only have to change the letters around to make the word *seal* into *sale*." For a word like *sea*, make sure they understand that it's the ocean, not *s-e-e*.

be	sea	ball	balls	labels
as	all	bell	bells	baseball
		sell	bales	
		seal/	label	
		sale		
		bale		
		base		

SORT FOR: b   s   ale   ell   s (plural)
baseball (compound word)

WRITING AND NEED TO SPELL:
yell (-ell)
(Perhaps they are writing about lunch in the cafeteria!)

Copyright © 1994, Good Apple

G1498

LETTERS:  a e b k s s t

WORDS TO MAKE:

Give children clues about how many letters to use and how many letters to change. "Now we're going to make some four-letter words. Hold up four fingers! Change just the first letter and you can change the word *sake* into *take*." For words like *steak/stake* which can be made from the same letters, tell the children, "Don't take any letters out. Just change the letters around and you can change *steak* into *stake*." For the homophones–*steak, stake*–give them meanings they might understand as you ask the children to make the words. "Mike always eats steak at his favorite restaurant. The wooden stake helps mark off the new lot."

as	bat	sake	beast	beasts	baskets
at	sat	take	steak/	skates	
		bake/	stake/	basket	
		beak	skate		

SORT FOR: b   s   at   ake   s (plural)
steak, stake (homophones)

WRITING AND NEED TO SPELL:
hat (-at)
flake (-ake)

(Perhaps they are writing about a snowstorm!)

Copyright © 1994, Good Apple

28

LETTERS:  a u b b h s t t

WORDS TO MAKE:

Give children clues about how many letters to use and how many letters to change. "Now we're going to make some three-letter words. Hold up three fingers! Change just the first letter and you can change the word *sub* into *tub*." For words like *bus/sub* which can be made from the same letters, tell the children, "Don't take any letters out. Just change the letters around and you can change the word *bus* into *sub*." For an unusual word like *tuba*, give them a meaning they might understand. "The boy played a tuba in the band."

as	bus/	that	bathtub
us	sub	bath	bathtubs
	tub/	stab	
	but	stub/	
	bat/	tubs	
	tab	tuba	
	hut		
	hat		

SORT FOR: b t h th at ab ub
bathtub (compound word)

WRITING AND NEED TO SPELL:

crab (-ab)

scrub (-ub)

(Perhaps they are writing about catching and cooking crabs!)

Copyright © 1994, Good Apple

LETTERS:  a e e b c h s

WORDS TO MAKE:

Give children clues about how many letters to use and how many letters to change. "Now we're going to make some four-letter words. Hold up four fingers. Change just the first letter and you can change the word *cash* into *bash*." For words like *cabs/scab* which can be made from the same letters, tell the children, "Don't take any letters out. Just change the letters around and you can change *cabs* into *scab*." For an unusual word like *ache*, give them a meaning they might understand. "The girl had a toothache after eating candy."

be	she	cabs/	aches/	**beaches**
	see	scab	chase	
	sea	cash	beach	
	ash/	bash		
	has	each/		
	cab	ache		

SORT FOR: b c ash s-es (plural)
see-sea (homophones)

WRITING AND NEED TO SPELL:
crash (-ash)

crashes (-es)

(Perhaps they are writing about auto racing!)

LETTERS:  i e b g g s t

WORDS TO MAKE:

Give children clues about how many letters to use and how many letters to change. "Now we're going to make some four-letter words. Hold up four fingers! Change just one letter and you can change the word *begs* into *bets*." For words like *bets/best* which can be made from the same letters, tell the children, "Don't take any letters out. Just change the letters around and you can change the word *bets* into the word *best*."

is	sit	eggs	bites	biggest
it	bit	begs		
	big	bets/		
	beg	best		
	bet	bite		
	set			
	get			
	egg			

SORT FOR: b it et s-pairs

WRITING AND NEED TO SPELL:

quit (-it)

pet (-et)

(Perhaps they are writing about taking care of a pet for a neighbor!)

Copyright © 1994, Good Apple

G1498

LETTERS:  a e b k l n t

A two-day lesson or pick and choose some words.
You may want to make all the words one day and sort/spell the next day.

WORDS TO MAKE:

Give children clues about how many letters to use and how many letters to change. "Now we're going to make some four-letter words. Hold up four fingers! Change just the first letter and you can change the word *beat* into *neat*." For words like *tan/ant* which can be made from the same letters, tell the children, "Don't take any letters out. Just change the letters around and you can change *tan* into *ant*." Also, alert the children when they should take all the letters out and start from scratch to make a new word. "Now take all the letters out and start over and make the four-letter word *lake*." For an unusual word like *ankle*, give them a meaning they might understand. "The boy tripped going down the steps and hurt his ankle."

at	ban	beat	blank	anklet	**blanket**
an	tan/	neat	bleak		
	ant	leak/	table		
	eat/	lake	ankle		
	ate/	bake			
	tea	take			
	ten	tank			
	Ben	bank			
	Ken				
	net				
	let				
	bet				

SORT FOR: b l bl
an   en   et   eat   ank   ake

WRITING AND NEED TO SPELL:

treat (-eat)

cake (-ake)

(Perhaps they are writing about a special dessert!)

Copyright © 1994, Good Apple

G1498

LETTERS:  a e i b g k n r

A two-day lesson or pick and choose some words.
You may want to make all the words one day and sort/spell the next day.

WORDS TO MAKE:

Give children clues about how many letters to use and how many letters to change. "Now we're going to make some four-letter words. Hold up four fingers! Change just the last letter and you can change the word *bang* into *bank*." For words like *break/brake* which can be made from the same letters, tell the children, "Don't take any letters out. Just change the letters around and you can change *break*, which means to crack into pieces, into *brake*, which is used to stop a car." Remember to give meanings to the other homophones in the lesson, *bear-bare*. Also, alert the children when they should take all the letters out and start from scratch to make a new word. "Now take all the letters out and start over and make the four-letter word *bike*."

be	beg	brag	brain	banker	barking
	bag	bang	break/	baking	bearing
	bar	bank	brake		braking
	rag	bare/	bring		**breaking**
		bear	being/		
		bike	begin		
		bake	began		
		bark	biker		
			baker		

SORT FOR: b   br   ag   ake
er (ending)   ing (ending)
bear-bare, break-brake (homophones)

(Help children to notice that the *e* in *bake* and *brake* is dropped when *ing* is added.)

WRITING AND NEED TO SPELL:

brag (-ag)
biking (-ing)

(Perhaps they are writing about what great bike riders they are!)

Copyright © 1994, Good Apple

G1498

LETTERS:  e i b d g r s

WORDS TO MAKE:

Give children clues about how many letters to use and how many letters to change. "Now we're going to make some four-letter words. Hold up four fingers! Change just the first letter and you can change the word *ride* into *side*." Alert the children when they should take all the letters out and start from scratch to make a new word. "Now take all the letters out and start over and make the three-letter word *dig*." Also, tell children adding just one letter changes a word. "Add one letter to *bird* and you have the plural, *birds*!"

Ed	red	ride	birds	ridges	**bridges**
	bed	side	bride	brides	
	big	beds	ridge	bridge	
	rig	bird			
	dig				
	rid				

SORT FOR: b r br ed ide idge
s (plural)

WRITING AND NEED TO SPELL:
Midge (-idge)

hide (-ide)

(Perhaps they are writing about a game of hide-and-seek!)

Copyright © 1994, Good Apple

G1498

LETTERS:  a a e c m r

WORDS TO MAKE:

Give children clues about how many letters to use and how many letters to change. "Now we're going to make some four-letter words. Hold up four fingers! Change just one letter and you can change the word *arm* into *arc*." Also, tell children adding just one letter will change one word into another. "Add one letter to *car* and you have a new four-letter word, *care!*" Alert the children when they should take all the letters out and start from scratch to make a new word. "Now take all the letters out and start over and make the four-letter word *area*."

am	ram/	care/	cream	camera
	arm	acre/		
	arc	race		
	are/	mace/		
	ear	came		
	ace	area		
	car	cram		

SORT FOR: c r cr am ace

WRITING AND NEED TO SPELL:

slam (-am)

place (-ace)

(Perhaps they are writing about a baseball game!)

LETTERS: 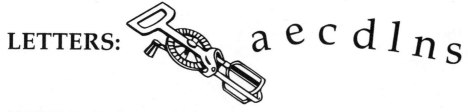 a e c d l n s

WORDS TO MAKE:

Give children clues about how many letters to use and how many letters to change. "Now we're going to make some two-letter words. Hold up two fingers! Change just the last letter and you can change the word *as* into *an*." For words like *Dan/and* which can be made from the same letters, tell the children, "Don't take any letters out. Just change the letters around and you can change *Dan* into the word *and*." For plural words like *dances* explain, "You just add one letter to *dance* and you have the plural *dances*. How many dances can you do?"

as	can	sand	clean	dances	**candles**
an	Dan/	land	laces	cleans	
	and	lace	dance	candle	
		clan			

SORT FOR: c l cl an and s-pairs

WRITING AND NEED TO SPELL:

       plan (-an)

       band (-and)

(Perhaps they are writing about a musical group they want to see!)

Copyright © 1994, Good Apple

G1498

LETTERS:  a e e c s s t t

WORDS TO MAKE:

Give children clues about how many letters to use and how many letters to change. "Now we're going to make some three-letter words. Hold up three fingers! Add just one letter and you can change the two-letter word *at* into a three-letter word, *cat*." For words like *cat/act* which can be made from the same letters, tell the children, "Don't take any letters out. Just change the letters around and you can change *cat* into *act*." Also, alert the children when they should take all the letters out and start from scratch to make a new word. "Now take all the letters out and start over and make the four-letter word *cast*." For an unusual word like *ease*, give them a meaning they might understand. "The little boy could ride his bike with ease."

as	cat/	seat/	state/	estate	**cassette**
at	act	east	taste		
	ate	ease	tease		
	sat	scat/			
	set	cast			
		test			

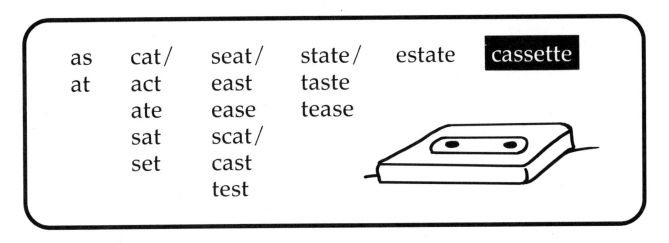

SORT FOR: c s at ate eat ease

WRITING AND NEED TO SPELL:

plate (-ate)

please (-ease)

(Perhaps they are writing about eating dinner!)

Copyright © 1994. Good Apple

G1498

LETTERS:  a e c l s s t

WORDS TO MAKE:

Give children clues about how many letters to use and how many letters to change. "Now we're going to make some three-letter words. Hold up three fingers! Change just one letter and you can change the word *cat* into *sat*." For words like *scat/cast* which can be made from the same letters, tell the children, "Don't take any letters out. Just change the letters around and you can change *scat* into *cast*." Also, alert the children when they should take all the letters out and start from scratch to make a new word. "Now take all the letters out and start over and make the five-letter word *class*." For an unusual word like *stale*, give them a meaning they might understand. "The bread was too stale to make a sandwich."

as	cat	eats/	least	scales	castles
at	sat	seat	class	castle	
	eat	sale	stale		
		scat/	scale		
		cast			
		last			

SORT FOR: c s at ast ale eat

WRITING AND NEED TO SPELL:

neat (-eat)

fast (-ast)

(Perhaps they are writing about cleaning up their rooms!)

LETTERS:  a e e c l r s

A two-day lesson or pick and choose some words.
You may want to make all the words one day and sort/spell the next day.

WORDS TO MAKE:

Give children clues about how many letters to use and how many letters to change. "Now we're going to make some three-letter words. Hold up three fingers! Change just one letter and you can change the word *sea*, the ocean, into *see*, with your eyes." Be sure to do the same thing for the homophones *real* and *reel*. For words like *are/ear* which can be made from the same letters, tell the children, "Don't take any letters out. Just change the letters around and you can change *are* into *ear*." Alert the children when they should take all the letters out and start from scratch to make a new word. "Now take all the letters out and start over and make the three-letter word *car*." For an unusual word like *acre*, give them a meaning they might understand. "The garden was on an acre lot."

Al	see	ears	scare/	crease	**cereals**
as	sea	acre	races/	sealer/	
	ace	race	cares	resale	
	car	lace	clear	cereal	
	are/	care	cease		
	ear	reel	lease		
		real	scale		
		seal/	acres		
		sale	erase		
		scar	easel		

CORN FLAKES GO POWER

OAT-MEAL

SORT FOR: c (car-cereal)   s   sc   ace
ease   ale
see-sea, reel-real (homophones)

WRITING AND NEED TO SPELL:

grease (-ease)

place (-ace)

(Perhaps they are writing about an auto mechanic!)

Copyright © 1994, Good Apple

G1498

LETTERS:  a i c h r s

WORDS TO MAKE:

Give children clues about how many letters to use and how many letters to change. "Now we're going to make some three-letter words. Hold up three fingers! Change just the vowel and you can change the word *his* into *has*." For words like *has/ash* which can be made from the same letters, tell the children, "Don't take any letters out. Just change the letters around and you can change the word *has* into the word *ash*." For an unusual word like *arch*, give them a meaning they might understand. "The golden arch is the symbol for McDonalds."

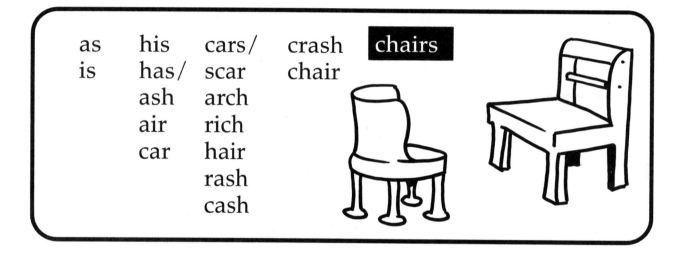

as	his	cars/	crash	**chairs**
is	has/	scar	chair	
	ash	arch		
	air	rich		
	car	hair		
		rash		
		cash		

SORT FOR: c h ch air ash s(plural)

WRITING AND NEED TO SPELL:

stair (-air)

smash (-ash)

(Perhaps they are writing about an accident.)

Copyright © 1994, Good Apple

G1498

LETTERS: 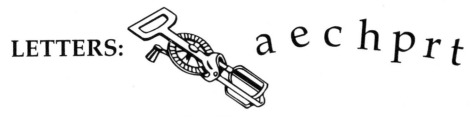 a e c h p r t

WORDS TO MAKE:

Give children clues about how many letters to use and how many letters to change. "Now we're going to make some three-letter words. Hold up three fingers! Change just the last letter of the word *car* and you can make the new word *cat*." For words like *cheat/teach*, which can be made from the same letters, tell the children, "Don't take any letters out. Just change the letters around and you can change *cheat* into *teach*."

at	eat	chat	cheap	preach	chapter
	art	cart	chart		
	car	heat	cheat/		
	cat	heap	teach		
	hat	each	peach		
			reach		

SORT FOR: c h ch at art eat each

WRITING AND NEED TO SPELL:

beat (-eat)

start (-art)

(Perhaps they are writing about a race!)

Copyright © 1994, Good Apple

LETTERS:  e e i c g h n r

WORDS TO MAKE:

Give children clues about how many letters to use and how many letters to change. "Now we're going to make some four-letter words. Hold up four fingers! Change just the first letter and you can change the word *nice* into *rice*." For words like *ring/grin*, which can be made from the same letters, tell the children, "Don't take any letters out. Just change the letters around and you can change *ring* into the new word *grin*." For an unusual word like *hinge*, give them a meaning they might understand. "The door was hanging by just one hinge."

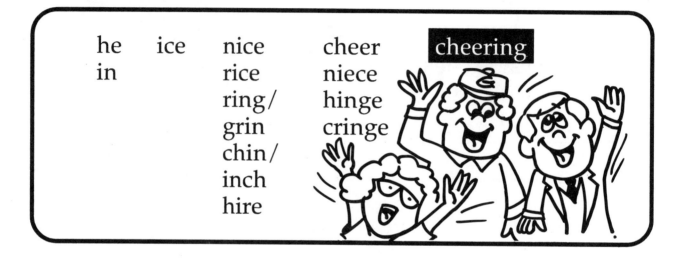

he	ice	nice	cheer	cheering
in		rice	niece	
		ring/	hinge	
		grin	cringe	
		chin/		
		inch		
		hire		

SORT FOR: h ch in ice inge

WRITING AND NEED TO SPELL:

> price (-ice)
> binge (-inge)

(Perhaps they are writing about a shopping spree!)

Copyright © 1994, Good Apple

G1498

LETTERS:  e i c c h k n s

WORDS TO MAKE:

Give children clues about how many letters to use and how many letters to change. "Now we're going to make some four-letter words. Hold up four fingers! Change just the first letter and you can change the word *heck* into *neck*." To change a word by changing the vowel sound say, "Change just the vowel and you can change the word *neck* into *nick*."

he	his	hens	chick	checks	chicken
is	hen	heck	check	chicks	**chickens**
		neck			
		nick			
		hick			
		sick			

SORT FOR: h ch eck ick s (plural)

WRITING AND NEED TO SPELL: pick (-ick) peck (-eck)

(Perhaps they are writing about chickens or grouchy children!)

LETTERS:  o u c d l s

WORDS TO MAKE:

Give children clues about how many letters to use and how many letters to change. "Now we're going to make some three-letter words. Hold up three fingers! Change just the first letter and you can change the word *sod* into *cod*." For words like *cold/clod* which can be made from the same letters, tell the children, "Don't take any letters out. Just change the letters around and you can change *cold* into the new word *clod*." For an unusual word like *cod*, give them a meaning they might understand, "My favorite fish to eat is cod."

do	sod	cold/	scold/	**clouds**
so	cod	clod	colds/	
	old	loud	clods	
		sold	could/	
			cloud	

SORT FOR: c cl od old oud s (plural)

WRITING AND NEED TO SPELL: told (-old) proud (-oud)

(Perhaps they are writing about their hero!)

Copyright © 1994. Good Apple

G1498

LETTERS:  e o u c m p r t

WORDS TO MAKE:

Give children clues about how many letters to use and how many letters to change. "Now we're going to make some three-letter words. Hold up three fingers! Change just the first letter and you can change the word *top* into *mop*," or "Change just the last letter in *cop* and you have a new word, *cot*." For an unusual word like *cot*, give them a meaning they might understand, "I slept on a little cot at the cabin last summer."

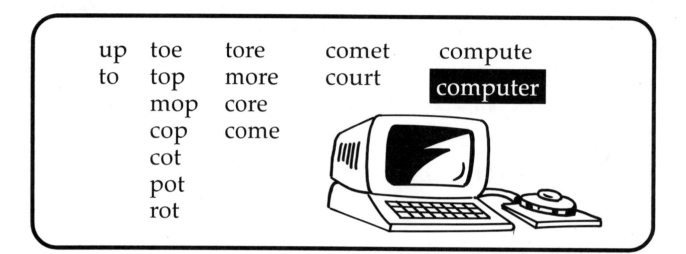

up	toe	tore	comet	compute
to	top	more	court	computer
	mop	core		
	cop	come		
	cot			
	pot			
	rot			

SORT FOR: c   op   ot   ore

WRITING AND NEED TO SPELL:

stop (-op)

shore (-ore)

(Perhaps they are writing about a trip to the beach!)

Copyright © 1994, Good Apple

G1498

LETTERS:  e o u c d n t

WORDS TO MAKE:

Give children clues about how many letters to use and how many letters to change. "Now we're going to make some three-letter words. Hold up three fingers! Change just the first letter and you can change the word *not* into *dot*." To add a letter and make four-letter words say, "When you add just one letter to the word *con* you can make the new word *cone*. For an unusual word like *con*, give them a meaning they might understand, "Don't let those men con you out of your money."

on/	not	cone	noted	counted
no	dot	cute	ounce	
	cot	dent	count	
	cut	once		
	nut	note		
	one			
	con			

SORT FOR: c   n   ot   ut

WRITING AND NEED TO SPELL:

shot (-ot)

shut (-ut)

(Perhaps they are writing about a robbery!)

Copyright © 1994, Good Apple

G1498

LETTERS:  o u c n r t y

WORDS TO MAKE:

Give children clues about how many letters to use and how many letters to change. "Now we're going to make some three-letter words. Hold up three fingers! Change just the first letter and you can change the word *rut* into *cut*." To add a letter and make a four-letter word say, "When you add just one letter to the word *you*, you can make the new word *your*. For an unusual word like *corny*, give them a meaning they might understand, "Everyone was laughing but the joke was corny."

on	toy	your	corny	county
to	coy	torn	court	country
	Roy	corn	count	
	rut			
	cut			
	nut			
	out			
	our			
	you			

SORT FOR: c   t   oy   ut   orn

WRITING AND NEED TO SPELL:

strut (-ut)

horn (-orn)

(Perhaps they are writing about a parade!)

Copyright © 1994, Good Apple

G1498

LETTERS: e o c r s v

WORDS TO MAKE:

Give children clues about how many letters to use and how many letters to change. "Now we're going to make some four-letter words. Hold up four fingers! Change just the first letter and you can change the word *core* into the new word *sore*." Be sure to give meanings for the homophones *or* and *ore*. For an unusual word like *rove*, give them a meaning they might understand, "The dog was allowed to rove over the farm."

so	ore	core	cores/
or		ores/	score
		sore/	cover
		rose	
		rove	
		cove	
		over	

covers

SORT FOR: c   r   ore   ove   s(plural)
or-ore (homophones)

WRITING AND NEED TO SPELL:

store (-ore)

drove (-ove)

(Perhaps they are writing about a trip to the mall!)

Copyright © 1994, Good Apple

LETTERS:  o o b c s w y

WORDS TO MAKE:

Give children clues about how many letters to use and how many letters to change. "Now we're going to make some three-letter words. Hold up three fingers! Change just the first letter in *boy* and you can change the word *boy* into *coy*." To change a word by adding one letter say, "Just add a letter to *cow* and you can make the plural, *cows*." For the many unusual words like *coy* and *soy*, give them a meaning they might understand, "The little girl was acting coy," or "I like soy sauce on Chinese food."

by	boy	cows	cowboy	cowboys
	coy	bows		
	soy	boys		
	sob			
	cob			
	coo			
	woo			
	boo			
	bow			
	sow			
	cow			

SORT FOR: c b oy oo ow s(plural)

(Help the children to notice that *bow-bows* and *sow* can be pronounced two ways and have two different meanings.)

WRITING AND NEED TO SPELL:

toy (-oy)

now (-ow)

(Perhaps they are writing about a holiday present!)

Copyright © 1994, Good Apple

G1498

LETTERS:  a e c c k r r s

WORDS TO MAKE:

Give children clues about how many letters to use and how many letters to change. "Now we're going to make some four-letter words. Hold up four fingers! Change just the first letter and you can change the word *care* into *rare*." For the words *car*, *scare*, and *cracks*, they may want to take all the letters out to make the new word. For unusual words like *creak*, give them a meaning they might understand, "The gate will creak when you open it."

as	ask	care	crack	cracks	cracker
	car	rare	creak		crackers
		rake	scare		
		cake			
		sake			
		sack			
		rack			

SORT FOR: c   r   cr   ake   ack   are

WRITING AND NEED TO SPELL:

black (-ack)

snake (-ake)

(Perhaps they are writing about reptiles!)

Copyright © 1994, Good Apple

LETTERS:  a e e u c r r t

WORDS TO MAKE:

Give children clues about how many letters to use and how many letters to change. "Now we're going to make some three-letter words. Hold up three fingers! Change just the first letter and you can change the word *rat* into *cat*." For words like *ate/eat* which can be made from the same letters, tell the children, "Don't take any letters out. Just change the letters around and you can change *ate* to *eat*." For unusual words, like *react*, give them a meaning they might understand, "Don't get mad and react without thinking."

at	rat	care	crate/	create	**creature**
	cat/	rare	react/	retrace	
	act	rate	trace		
	ate/	rear			
	eat	tear			
	ear/				
	are				

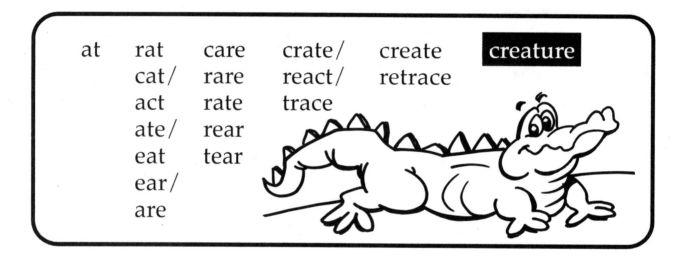

SORT FOR: c r cr at ate ear
re (react, retrace)

(Help the children to notice that *tear* has two pronunciations and two meanings.)

WRITING AND NEED TO SPELL:

late (-ate)

fear (-ear)

(Perhaps they are writing about being late for school!)

Copyright © 1994, Good Apple

G1498

LETTERS:  a e c d n s

WORDS TO MAKE:

Give children clues about how many letters to use and how many letters to change. "Now we're going to make some four-letter words. Hold up four fingers! Change just the last letter and you can change the word *cans* into *cane*." To change a word by changing the vowel, say, "Change the vowel and you can change the word *sand* into *send*." For words like *and/Dan* which can be made from the same letters, tell the children, "Don't take any letters out. Just change the letters around and you can change *and* into *Dan*." For unusual words like *sedan*, give them a meaning they might understand. "Mom's new car is a sedan."

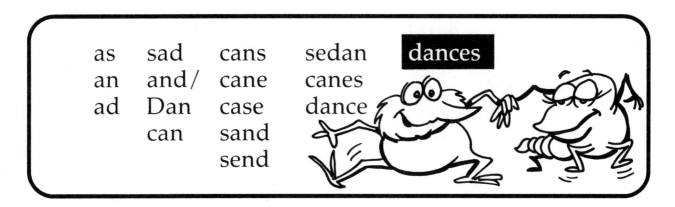

as	sad	cans	sedan	dances
an	and/	cane	canes	
ad	Dan	case	dance	
	can	sand		
		send		

SORT FOR: c   d   s   ad   an   and   s (plural)

WRITING AND NEED TO SPELL:
glad (-ad)
band (-and)

(Perhaps they are writing about a parade!)

Copyright © 1994. Good Apple

G1498

LETTERS:  a i d g l n r

WORDS TO MAKE:

Give children clues about how many letters to use and how many letters to change. "Now we're going to make some five-letter words. Hold up five fingers! Change just the first letter and you can change the word *grain* into *drain*." For words like *Dan/and* which can be made from the same letters, tell the children, "Don't take any letters out. Just change the letters around and you can change *Dan* into *and*." For unusual words, like *daring*, give them a meaning they might understand, "The girl was daring and rode her bike straight down the steep hill."

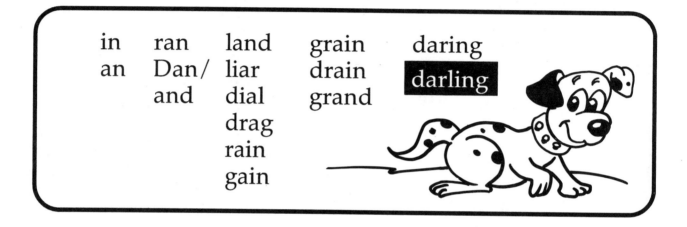

in	ran	land	grain	daring
an	Dan/	liar	drain	darling
	and	dial	grand	
		drag		
		rain		
		gain		

SORT FOR: d dr gr an and ain

WRITING AND NEED TO SPELL:

land (-and)

train (-ain)

(Perhaps they are writing about a train trip!)

Copyright © 1994, Good Apple

52

G1498

LETTERS:  a e u d g h r t

WORDS TO MAKE:

Give children clues about how many letters to use and how many letters to change. "Now we're going to make some three-letter words. Hold up three fingers! Change just the first letter and you can change the word *rat* into *hat*." To change a word by changing the vowel, say, "Change the vowel and you can change the word *rag* into *rug*." For words like *art/rat* which can be made from the same letters, tell the children, "Don't take any letters out. Just change the letters around and you can change *art* into a new word, *rat*."

at	art/	drug	heart	thread
	rat	drag	heard	daughter
	hat	dart	earth	
	rag			
	rug			
	hug			
	dug			

SORT FOR: d   r   dr   at   ug   art

WRITING AND NEED TO SPELL:

bug (-ug)

start (-art)

(Perhaps they are writing about a bug race!)

Copyright © 1994, Good Apple

G1498

LETTERS:  e i d n n r

WORDS TO MAKE:

Give children clues about how many letters to use and how many letters to change. "Now we're going to make some three-letter words. Hold up three fingers! Change the vowel and you can change the word *red* into *rid*." For words like *end/den* which can be made from the same letters, tell the children, "Don't take any letters out. Just change the letters around and you can change *end* into a new word, *den*." For unusual words like *rind*, give them a meaning they might understand, "I ate everything but the watermelon rind." Also, remember to give the children the meanings of the two homophones *in* and *inn* when asking them to make those words.

Ed	inn	ride	diner	**dinner**
in	die	rind		
	end/	rein		
	den/	nine		
	Ned	dine		
	red			
	rid			

SORT FOR: d r ed ine names
in-inn (homophones)

WRITING AND NEED TO SPELL:
Ted (-ed)

mine (-ine)

(Perhaps they are writing about sharing with their friends!)

Copyright © 1994. Good Apple

54

LETTERS:  o o c d r t

WORDS TO MAKE:

Give children clues about how many letters to use and how many letters to change. "Now we're going to make some three-letter words. Hold up three fingers! Change just the first letter and you can change the word *dot* into *cot*." For words like *door/odor* which can be made from the same letters, tell the children, "Don't take any letters out. Just change the letters around and you can change *door* into *odor*." For unusual words like *trod*, give them a meaning they might understand, "The boy trod down the road to school." Also, remember to give the meanings of the homophones *to* and *too* when asking children to make those words.

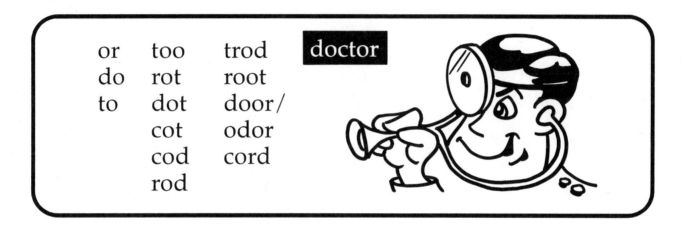

or	too	trod	doctor
do	rot	root	
to	dot	door/	
	cot	odor	
	cod	cord	
	rod		

SORT FOR: d od ot to-too (homophones)

WRITING AND NEED TO SPELL:

> clod (-od)
>
> trot (-ot)

(Perhaps they are writing about a monster!)

Copyright © 1994, Good Apple

G1498

LETTERS:  e o o b d l l r

WORDS TO MAKE:

Give children clues about how many letters to use and how many letters to change. "Now we're going to make some four-letter words. Hold up four fingers! Change just one letter and you can change the word *roll*, to roll down a hill, into *role*, like the role in a play." For words like *bored/robed* which can be made from the same letters, tell the children, "Don't take any letters out. Just change the letters around and you can change *bored* into *robed*." Also, talk about the compound words *bedroll* and *doorbell* as the children make them. Remind the children that they are made up of two small words they just made.

be	red	bled	bored/	rolled	bedroll
Ed	bed	bell	robed		**doorbell**
		door	older		
		roll			
		role			
		robe/			
		bore			

SORT FOR:
r   ed   ed (ending)
roll-role (homophones)
bedroll, doorbell (compound words)

WRITING AND NEED TO SPELL:

fed (-ed)

wed (-ed)

(Perhaps they are writing about a wedding!)

LETTERS:  a e d m r s

WORDS TO MAKE:

Give children clues about how many letters to use and how many letters to change. "Now we're going to make some two-letter words. Hold up two fingers! Change just the last letter and you can change the word *as* into *am*." For words like *ram/arm* which can be made from the same letters, tell the children, "Don't take any letters out. Just change the letters around and you can change *ram* to *arm*."

as	Sam	made	smear	dreams
am	ram/	rams/	reads/	
	arm	arms	dares	
	ear	read/	dream	
	mad	dare/		
		dear		

SORT FOR: d   dr   am   ear   s-pairs

WRITING AND NEED TO SPELL:

fear (-ear)

spear (-ear)

(Perhaps they are writing about a fight!)

Copyright © 1994, Good Apple

G1498

LETTERS: 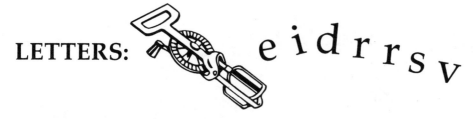 e i d r r s v

WORDS TO MAKE:

Give children clues about how many letters to use and how many letters to change. "Now we're going to make some four-letter words. Hold up four fingers! Change just the first letter and you can change the word *side* into *ride*." For words like *rider/drier* which can be made from the same letters, tell the children, "Don't take any letters out. Just change the letters around and you can change *rider* to *drier*." For unusual words, like *rise*, give them a meaning they might understand, "The bread dough will rise."

is	sir	dive	river	driver
	red	side	rider/	drivers
	die	ride	drier	
		rise	drive/	
			diver	

SORT FOR: d   dr   ide   ive   er (river-rider)

(Pull out all the *er* words. Then help the children sort them into the ones in which the *er* means the person who does something.)

WRITING AND NEED TO SPELL:

bride (-ide)

five (-ive)

(Perhaps they are writing about a wedding!)

Copyright © 1994, Good Apple

G1498

LETTERS:  *i u c d g k l n*

WORDS TO MAKE:

Give children clues about how many letters to use and how many letters to change. "Now we're going to make some three-letter words. Hold up three fingers! Change just the first letter and you can change the word *kid* into *lid*." To change a word by changing the vowel sound say, "Change just the vowel and you can change the word *luck* into *lick*." For words like *kin/ink* which can be made from the same letters, tell the children, "Don't take any letters out. Just change the letters around and you can change *kin* to *ink*." For unusual words like *clung*, give them a meaning they might understand, "The little boy clung to his puppy."

in	kin/	duck	clunk	ducking
	ink	luck	clink	duckling
	kid	lick	cling	
	lid	Nick	clung	
	dig	Dick		
	dug	dunk		
		gunk		

SORT FOR: d l cl id ick uck unk
names

WRITING AND NEED TO SPELL:
junk (-unk)
truck (-uck)

(Perhaps they are writing about moving or a very old truck!)

LETTERS: 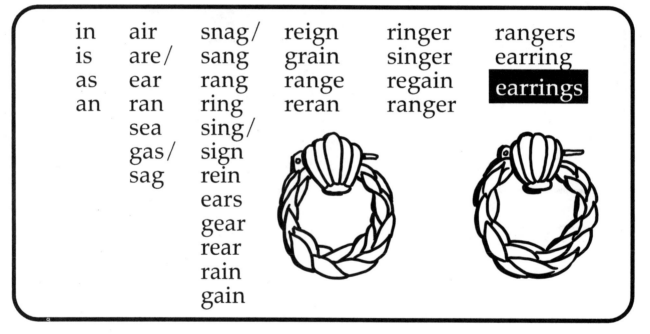 a e i g n r r s

A two-day lesson or pick and choose some words.
You may want to make all words one day and sort/spell the next day.

WORDS TO MAKE:

Give children clues about how many letters to use and how many letters to change.
"Now we're going to make some four-letter words. Hold up four fingers! Change just
the vowel and you can change the word *rang* into *ring*. Change just the first letter and
you can change *ringer* to the new word *singer*." Also alert the children when they
should take all the letters out and start from scratch to make a new word. "Now take all
the letters out and start over and make the word *rein*." For words like *sag/gas* which can
be made from the same letters, tell the children, "Don't take any letters out. Just change
the letters around and you can change *gas* to *sag*." For unusual words like *reign*, give
them a meaning they might understand, "The king will reign over the kingdom."
Remember to give the meaning of all three homophones when making those words.
You might also give the meaning when making *reran* and *regain*.

in	air	snag/	reign	ringer	rangers
is	are/	sang	grain	singer	earring
as	ear	rang	range	regain	**earrings**
an	ran	ring	reran	ranger	
	sea	sing/			
	gas/	sign			
	sag	rein			
		ears			
		gear			
		rear			
		rain			
		gain			

SORT FOR: s   r   ear   ain   er (ending)
re (reran) rain-rein-reign (homophones)

WRITING AND NEED TO SPELL:

smear (-ear)

stain (-ain)

(Perhaps they are writing about painting a house!)

Copyright © 1994, Good Apple

G1498

LETTERS:  a e e h l p n t

WORDS TO MAKE:

Give children clues about how many letters to use and how many letters to change. "Now we're going to make some four-letter words. Hold up four fingers! Change just the first letter and you can change the word *heel* into *peel*. Change just the vowel and you can change *pan* to *pen*." Also, alert the children when they should take all the letters out and start from scratch to make a new word. "Now take all the letters out and start over and make the word *plan*." Give them meanings for the homophones before they make them. "A bell peals but you peel a banana." For an unusual word like *peat*, give them a meaning they might understand. "The gardener put peat around the flower beds."

at	tan	heal	plane	planet
an	pan	heel	plate/	elephant
	pen	peel	pleat	
	hen	peal	plant	
	ten	peat		
		plan		

SORT FOR: p pl an en e (ee-ea)
peel-peal (homophones)

WRITING AND NEED TO SPELL:

van (-an)

men (-en)

(Perhaps they are writing about moving or a trip!)

LETTERS:  e e i g n n s

WORDS TO MAKE:

Give children clues about how many letters to use and how many letters to change. "Now we're going to make some four-letter words. Hold up four fingers!" For words like *sing/sign* which can be made from the same letters, tell the children, "Don't take any letters out. Just change the letters around and you can change *sing* into *sign*." Alert the children when they should take all the letters out and start from scratch to make a new word. "Now take all the letters out and start over and make the word *seeing*." Also, remember to give the meanings of the homophones *in* and *inn* when asking the children to make those words.

is	inn	seen	nines	seeing	engines
in	sin	sing/		engine	
	see	sign			
		inns			
		nine			

SORT FOR: s   in   s (plural)   in-inn (homophones)

WRITING AND NEED TO SPELL:

        spin (-in)

        win (-in)

(Perhaps they are writing about playing a favorite board game!)

Copyright © 1994, Good Apple

G1498

LETTERS:  a e f m r r s

WORDS TO MAKE:

Give children clues about how many letters to use and how many letters to change. "Now we're going to make some four-letter words. Hold up four fingers! Change just the first letter and you can change the word *fear* into *rear*." For words like *ram/arm* which can be made from the same letters, tell the children, "Don't take any letters out. Just change the letters around and you can change *ram* into *arm*." Also, alert the children when they should take all the letters out and start from scratch to make a new word. "Now take all the letters out and start over and make the five-letter word *smear*." For an unusual word like *smear*, give them a meaning they might understand. "Don't smear the paint on everything."

me	Sam	fear	smear	frames	**farmers**
am	ram/	rear	frame	farmer	
	arm	farm			
	ear	fame			
		same			

SORT FOR: f r fr am ame ear
s (plural)

WRITING AND NEED TO SPELL:

flame (-ame)
flames (-s)

(Perhaps they are writing about a fire!)

Copyright © 1994, Good Apple

G1498

LETTERS:  a e e f h r s t

WORDS TO MAKE:

Give children clues about how many letters to use and how many letters to change. "Now we're going to make some four-letter words. Hold up four fingers! Change just one letter and you can change the word *seat* into the word *heat*." Also, alert the children when they should take all the letters out and start from scratch to make a new word. "Now take all the letters out and start over and make the word *sheet*." For the homophones *feat* and *feet*, give them a meaning they might understand when asking children to make these words. "Winning the race was quite a feat because she ran in her bare feet."

at	her	seat	heart	father	feathers
he	hat	heat	sheet	fathers	
	rat	feat	these	feather	
	sat	feet			

SORT FOR: f h at eat eet
feet-feat (homophones)

(Help the children to notice that words ending in *eat* and *eet* usually rhyme.)

WRITING AND NEED TO SPELL:

Pat (-at)

brat (-at)

(Perhaps they are writing about a spoiled neighbor!)

Copyright © 1994, Good Apple

G1498

LETTERS:  i i f g h n s

WORDS TO MAKE:

Give children clues about how many letters to use and how many letters to change. "Now we're going to make some four-letter words. Hold up four fingers! Change just one letter and you can change the word *figs* into *fins*." For words like *sign/sing* which can be made from the same letters, tell the children, "Don't take any letters out. Just change the letters around and you can change *sing* into *sign*." Also, alert the children when they should take all the letters out and start from scratch to make a new word. "Now take all the letters out and start over and make the six-letter word *finish*." For an unusual word like *sigh*, give them a meaning they might understand. "They gave a sigh of relief when the job was finished."

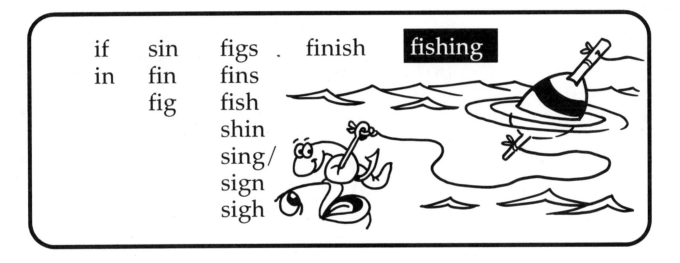

if	sin	figs	finish	**fishing**
in	fin	fins		
	fig	fish		
		shin		
		sing/		
		sign		
		sigh		

SORT FOR: f   in   s (plural)

WRITING AND NEED TO SPELL:

> twin (-in)
>
> signs (-s)

(Perhaps they are writing about twins who are having a yard sale!)

Copyright © 1994, Good Apple

LETTERS:  e o f l r s w

WORDS TO MAKE:

Give children clues about how many letters to use and how many letters to change. "Now we're going to make some three-letter words. Hold up three fingers! Change just one letter and you can change the word *owl* into *owe*." For words like *low/owl* which can be made from the same letters, tell the children, "Don't take any letters out. Just change the letters around and you can change *low* into *owl*." Also, alert the children when they should take all the letters out and start from scratch to make a new word. "Now take all the letters out and start over and make the word *slow*." For an unusual word like *fowl*, give them a meaning they might understand. "The men were out hunting for fowl." Remember to give the meanings for the homophones *rows* and *rose* as you ask the children to make those words.

so	few	flow/	lower	slower	flowers
we	low/	fowl		flower	
	owl	rows			
	owe	rose			
	row	slow/			
		owls			

SORT FOR: f l fl ow s (plural)
rose-rows (homophones)

(Help the children to notice the two common sounds for *ow*.)

WRITING AND NEED TO SPELL:

crow (-ow)

roses (-s)

(Perhaps they are writing about a garden or someone's backyard!)

Copyright © 1994. Good Apple

G1498

LETTERS:  a e e o d f h r

WORDS TO MAKE:

Give children clues about how many letters to use and how many letters to change. "Now we're going to make some four-letter words. Hold up four fingers! Change just one letter and you can change the word *dear* into the word *fear*." For words like *free/reef* which can be made from the same letters, tell the children, "Don't take any letters out. Just change the letters around and you can change *free* into *reef*." Remember to give the meanings for the homophones *read-reed* and *deer-dear* as you ask the children to make those words.

Ed	had	dear	feared	forehead
ad	fad	fear		
	fed	hear		
	red	read		
	ear	reed		
		reef/		
		free		
		deer		
		head		

SORT FOR: f h r ad ed ear
deer-dear, read-reed (homophones)

WRITING AND NEED TO SPELL:
glad (-ad)

mad (-ad)

(Perhaps they are writing about different ways people feel!)

Copyright © 1994, Good Apple

LETTERS:  e i d f n r s

WORDS TO MAKE:

Give children clues about how many letters to use and how many letters to change. "Now we're going to make some four-letter words. Hold up four fingers! Change just one letter and you can change the word *fire* into *fine*." For words like *fried/fired* which can be made from the same letters, tell the children, "Don't take any letters out. Just change the letters around and you can change *fried* into *fired*." Also, alert the children when they should take all the letters out and start from scratch to make a new word. "Now take all the letters out and start over and make the five-letter word *fried*." For an unusual word like *fired*, give them a meaning they might understand. "The art teacher fired the clay pot to harden it."

if	fin	fire	fried/	friend	**friends**
in	sin	fine	fired		
	sir	find	fires/		
	fir		fries		

SORT FOR: f   fr   in   ir   i (in / fine / sir)

WRITING AND NEED TO SPELL:

tin (-in)

stir (-ir)

(Perhaps they are writing about baking!)

Copyright © 1994, Good Apple

G1498

LETTERS:  a i g n s t

WORDS TO MAKE:

Give children clues about how many letters to use and how many letters to change. "Now we're going to make some three-letter words. Hold up three fingers! Change just one letter and you can change the word *nag* into the word *tag*." For words like *sag/gas* which can be made from the same letters, tell the children, "Don't take any letters out. Just change the letters around and you can change *sag* into *gas*." Also, alert the children when they should take all the letters out and start from scratch to make a new word. "Now take all the letters out and start over and make the word *gain*." For an unusual word like *stag*, give them a meaning they might understand. "A male deer is called a stag."

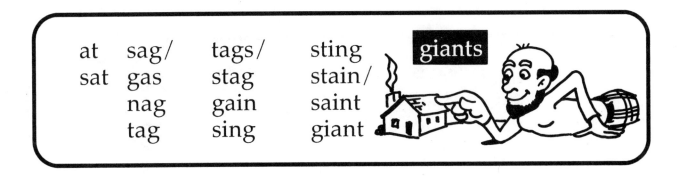

at	sag/	tags/	sting	giants
sat	gas	stag	stain/	
	nag	gain	saint	
	tag	sing	giant	

SORT FOR: g (gas/giant) s t st ag ain

WRITING AND NEED TO SPELL:

   bag (-ag)
   rain (-ain)

(Perhaps they are writing about a rainy day shopping trip!)

Copyright © 1994, Good Apple

G1498

LETTERS:  a e g l s s s

WORDS TO MAKE:

Give children clues about how many letters to use and how many letters to change. "Now we're going to make some four-letter words. Hold up four fingers! Change just one letter and you can change the word *seas* into *seal*." For words like *seal/sale* which can be made from the same letters, tell the children, "Don't take any letters out. Just change the letters around and you can change *seal* into *sale*." Also, alert the children when they should take all the letters out and start from scratch to make a new word. "Now take all the letters out and start over and make the word *glass*." For an unusual word like *lasses*, give them a meaning they might understand. "The young girls did not like being called lasses."

as	gas/ sag gal/ lag sea	seas seal/ sale legs lass	glass seals/ sales	lasses	**glasses**

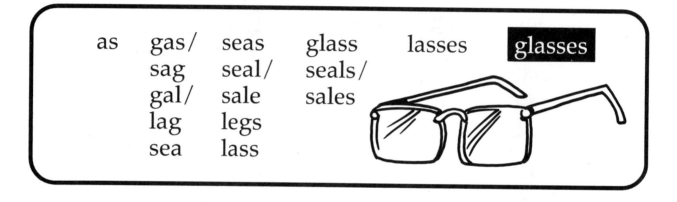

SORT FOR: g l gl s ag ass s/es (plural)

WRITING AND NEED TO SPELL:
> brag (-ag)
>
> pass (-ass)

(Perhaps they are writing about a football game!)

Copyright © 1994, Good Apple

G1498

LETTERS:  e o b g l s

WORDS TO MAKE:

Give children clues about how many letters to use and how many letters to change. "Now we're going to make some four-letter words. Hold up four fingers! Change just the vowel and you can change the word *legs* into *logs*." For words like *lobs/slob* which can be made from the same letters, tell the children, "Don't take any letters out. Just change the letters around and you can change *lobs* into *slob*." Also, alert the children when they should take all the letters out and start from scratch to make a new word. "Now take all the letters out and start over and make the word *seals*." For an unusual word like *lob*, give them a meaning they might understand. "The player will lob the tennis ball over the net."

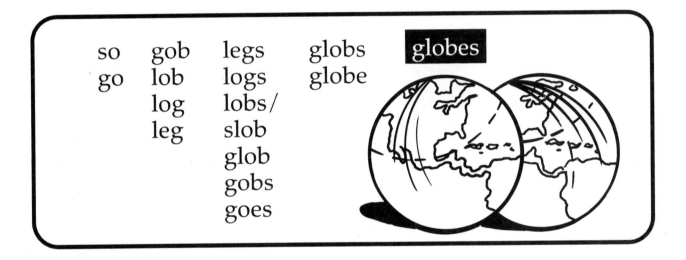

so	gob	legs	globs	**globes**
go	lob	logs	globe	
	log	lobs/		
	leg	slob		
		glob		
		gobs		
		goes		

SORT FOR: g l gl ob s (plural)

WRITING AND NEED TO SPELL:

> job (-ob)
>
> jobs (s-plural)

(Perhaps they are writing about what they want to be when they grow up!)

Copyright © 1994, Good Apple

G1498

LETTERS:  e o d g l n

WORDS TO MAKE:

Give children clues about how many letters to use and how many letters to change. "Now we're going to make some two-letter words. Hold up two fingers! Just change the first letter in the word *go* and you can make the word *no*." For words like *no/on* which can be made from the same letters, tell the children, "Don't take any letters out. Just change the letters around and you can change *no* into *on*." Also, alert the children when they should take all the letters out and start from scratch to make a new word. "Now take all the letters out and start over and make the word *end*." For an unusual word like *lodge*, give them a meaning they might understand. "The mountain lodge is a beautiful place for a vacation."

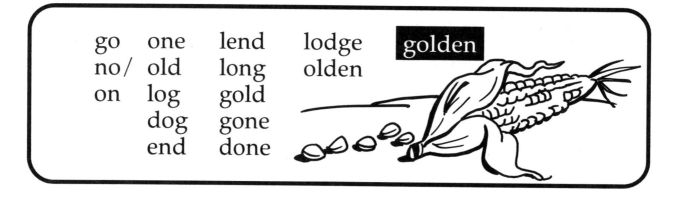

go	one	lend	lodge	golden
no/	old	long	olden	
on	log	gold		
	dog	gone		
	end	done		

SORT FOR: g   l   og   old   en (ending)

WRITING AND NEED TO SPELL:

　　　smog (-og)

　　　cold (-old)

(Perhaps they are writing about the weather!)

Copyright © 1994, Good Apple

G1498

LETTERS:  i o d f g h l s

WORDS TO MAKE:

Give children clues about how many letters to use and how many letters to change. "Now we're going to make some four-letter words. Hold up four fingers! Change just the first letter and you can change the word *soil* into *foil*." Alert the children when they should take all the letters out and start from scratch to make a new word. "Now take all the letters out and start over and make the four-letter word *hold*." For an unusual word like *golfs*, give them a meaning they might understand. "The woman golfs every Saturday morning."

go	dog	soil	golfs	**goldfish**
	old	foil	folds	
	oil	fish	holds	
		dish		
		hold		
		fold		
		sold		
		gold		
		golf		

SORT FOR: f g oil old s-pairs (golf-golfs)
goldfish (compound)

WRITING AND NEED TO SPELL:

scold (-old)

spoil (-oil)

(Perhaps they are writing about a time they got in trouble!)

Copyright © 1994, Good Apple

LETTERS:  e i g h l n p

WORDS TO MAKE:

Give children clues about how many letters to use and how many letters to change. "Now we're going to make some three-letter words. Hold up three fingers! Change just the first letter and you can change the word *hen* into *pen*." For words like *nip/pin* which can be made from the same letters, tell the children, "Don't take any letters out. Just change the letters around and you can change *nip* into *pin*." Also, alert the children when they should take all the letters out and start from scratch to make a new word. "Now take all the letters out and start over and make the five-letter word *hinge*." For an unusual word like *hinge*, give them a meaning they might understand. "The gate was hanging on just one hinge."

he   hen   line   hinge   helping
        pen   pine
        pig   help
        peg
        leg
        lip
        hip
        nip/
        pin
        pie
        lie

SORT FOR: h p l en eg ip ie ine

WRITING AND NEED TO SPELL:
slip (-ip)

spine (-ine)

(Perhaps they are writing about a bad fall!)

Copyright © 1994, Good Apple

74

LETTERS:  i u g h n n t

WORDS TO MAKE:

Give children clues about how many letters to use and how many letters to change. "Now we're going to make some four-letter words. Hold up four fingers! Change just one letter and you can change the word *hung* into *hunt*." For words like *hint/thin* which can be made from the same letters, tell the children, "Don't take any letters out. Just change the letters around and you can change *hint* into *thin*." Alert the children when they should take all the letters out and start from scratch to make a new word. "Now take all the letters out and start over and make the four-letter word *unit*." For an unusual word like *thug*, give them a meaning they might understand. "The police called the robber a thug." Also, remember to give the meanings for the homophones *in* and *inn* when asking the children to make those words.

it	inn	hung	thing/	hunting
in	tin	hunt	night	
	tug	thug	ninth	
	hug	unit		
		hint/		
		thin		

SORT FOR: t h th in ug
in-inn (homophones)

WRITING AND NEED TO SPELL:

spin (-in)

rug (-ug)

(Perhaps they are writing about playing a board game!)

Copyright © 1994, Good Apple

G1498

LETTERS:  a i d l n s s

WORDS TO MAKE:

Give children clues about how many letters to use and how many letters to change. "Now we're going to make some four-letter words. Hold up four fingers! Change just the first letter and you can change the word *land* into the word *sand*." For words like *sad/ads* which can be made from the same letters, tell the children, "Don't take any letters out. Just change the letters around and you can change *sad* into *ads*." For an unusual word like *snail*, give them a meaning they might understand. "The snail crawled through the garden."

is	lad	land	snail/	islands
in	sad/	sand	nails	
an	ads	said		
ad	and	sail		
		nail		

SORT FOR: s   ad   and   ail

WRITING AND NEED TO SPELL:
hand (-and)

tail (-ail)

(Perhaps they are writing about monkeys!)

Copyright © 1994, Good Apple

LETTERS:  i u g j m n p

WORDS TO MAKE:

Give children clues about how many letters to use and how many letters to change. "Now we're going to make some three-letter words. Hold up three fingers! Change just the vowel and you can change the word *pun* into *pin*." For words like *pin/nip* which can be made from the same letters, tell the children, "Don't take any letters out. Just change the letters around and you can change *pin* into *nip*." For an unusual word like *imp*, give them a meaning they might understand. "Most people called the mischievous girl an imp."

in   pun   jump   jumping
up   pin/
      nip
      imp
      pig
      jig
      jug
      pug
      mug/
      gum
      gun

SORT FOR: j   p   in   ig   ug   un

WRITING AND NEED TO SPELL:

dig (-ig)

bug (-ug)

(Perhaps they are writing about insects!)

Copyright © 1994, Good Apple

G1498

LETTERS:  e u g j l n s

WORDS TO MAKE:

Give children clues about how many letters to use and how many letters to change. "Now we're going to make some four-letter words. Hold up four fingers! Change just the second letter and you can change the word *snug* into *slug*." For words like *sung/snug* which can be made from the same letters, tell the children, "Don't take any letters out. Just change the letters around and you can change *sung* into *snug*." Also, alert the children when they should take all the letters out and start from scratch to make a new word. "Now take all the letters out and start over and make the word *glue*." For an unusual word like *slug*, give them a meaning they might understand. "A slug is a snail without a shell."

us	use	sung/	glues	jungle	jungles
	jug	snug	slung		
	lug	slug			
	gun	lung			
	sun	glue			

SORT FOR: j   ug   un   ung

WRITING AND NEED TO SPELL:

      run (-un)

      stung (-ung)

(Perhaps they are writing about bees or yellow jackets!)

Copyright © 1994, Good Apple

G1498

LETTERS:  a e o b d k r y

A two-day lesson or pick and choose some words.
You may want to make all words one day and sort/spell the next day.

WORDS TO MAKE:

Give children clues about how many letters to use and how many letters to change. "Now we're going to make some four-letter words. Hold up four fingers! Change just the first letter and you can change the word *bake* into *rake*." For words like *baker/brake/break* which can be made from the same letters, tell the children, "Don't take any letters out. Just change the letters around and you can change *baker* into *brake* and then *break*." Be sure to give a sentence with meanings for these homophones and all others in the lesson. When they make *read*, tell them both pronunciations.

or	doe	boar	ready	bakery
ad	day	bore	board	keyboard
do	ray	yoke	bored	
	red	okay	baker/	
	bed	bray	brake/	
	bad	bark	break	
	bay	bake		
	rye	rake		
	Roy	rode		
	boy	road		
	key	read		
	Kay/			
	yak			
	oar			
	ore			

SORT FOR: b br r y ay ed oy ake
names   homophones: or-oar-ore, boar-bore, board-bored, red-read, break-brake, road-rode

WRITING AND NEED TO SPELL:
play (-ay)
toy (-oy)

(Perhaps they are writing about what they do after school!)

Copyright © 1994, Good Apple

G1498

LETTERS:  e i c h k n s t

A two-day lesson or pick and choose some words.
You may want to make all words one day and sort/spell the next day.

WORDS TO MAKE:

Give children clues about how many letters to use and how many letters to change. "Now we're going to make some four-letter words. Hold up four fingers! Change just the last letter and you can change the word *skit* into the word *skin*." For words like *skin/sink* which can be made from the same letters, tell the children, "Don't take any letters out. Just change the letters around and you can change *skin* into *sink*." Also, alert the children when they should take all the letters out and start from scratch to make a new word. "Now take all the letters out and start over and make the word *ices*."

is	hit	skit	thick	sketch	thicken
in	sit	skin/	think	insect	kitchen
it	kit	sink/	chins	inches	kitchens
	kin	inks	chest		
	tin	inch/			
	ink	chin			
	ice	thin			
	ski	tick			
		ices			
		kite			
		knit			

SORT FOR: s k sk it in ink s/es (plural)

WRITING AND NEED TO SPELL:

blink (-ink)

wink (-ink)

(Perhaps they are writing about their eyes!)

Copyright © 1994, Good Apple

G1498

LETTERS:  e i k n s t t

WORDS TO MAKE:

Give children clues about how many letters to use and how many letters to change. "Now we're going to make some four-letter words. Hold up four fingers! Change just the first letter and you can change the word *tent* into the word *sent*." For words like *sink/skin* which can be made from the same letters, tell the children, "Don't take any letters out. Just change the letters around and you can change *sink* into *skin*." Also, alert the children when they should take all the letters out and start from scratch to make a new word. "Now take all the letters out and start over and make the five-letter word *tents*." For an unusual word like *skit*, give them a meaning they might understand. "The children made up a skit for the story."

in	sit	tent	kites	kitten	kittens
is	kit	sent	tents		
it	kin	sink/			
	Ken	skin			
	ten	skit			
		kite			

SORT FOR: k s sk it in s (plural)

WRITING AND NEED TO SPELL:

hit (-it)

win (-in)

(Perhaps they are writing about a baseball game!)

Copyright © 1994, Good Apple

G1498

LETTERS:  a e u d g h l

WORDS TO MAKE:

Give children clues about how many letters to use and how many letters to change. "Now we're going to make some three-letter words. Hold up three fingers! Change just the first letter and you can change the word *had* into the word *lad*." Alert the children when they should take all the letters out and start from scratch to make a new word. "Now take all the letters out and start over and make the word *glue*." For an unusual word like *haul*, give them a meaning they might understand. "We loaded the truck to haul the trash to the dump."

ad	had	huge	glued	hauled
ha	lad	haul	laugh	laughed
	lag	heal		
	lug	glad		
	dug	glue		
	hug			

SORT FOR: l   gl   ad   ug   ed (ending)

WRITING AND NEED TO SPELL:

dad (-ad)

snug (-ug)

(Perhaps they are writing about their fathers!)

Copyright © 1994, Good Apple

G1498

LETTERS:  i g h l s t

WORDS TO MAKE:

Give children clues about how many letters to use and how many letters to change. "Now we're going to make some three-letter words. Hold up three fingers! Change just the first letter and you can change the word *hit* into the word *lit*." For words like *sit/its* which can be made from the same letters, tell the children, "Don't take any letters out. Just change the letters around and you can change *sit* into *its*." For an unusual word like *slit*, give them a meaning they might understand. "The skirt had a slit in the back."

is	hit	hits/	sight	slight/
it	lit	this	light	lights
	sit/	list/		
	its	slit		
	his	sigh		

SORT FOR: l s sl it ight s-pairs (it/its)

WRITING AND NEED TO SPELL:

flit (-it)

bright (-ight)

(Perhaps they are writing about butterflies or lightning bugs!)

Copyright © 1994, Good Apple   G1498

LETTERS:  a i d l r s z

WORDS TO MAKE:

Give children clues about how many letters to use and how many letters to change. "Now we're going to make some four-letter words. Hold up four fingers! Change just the vowel and you can change the word *lids* into the word *lads*." For words like *liar/rail* which can be made from the same letters, tell the children, "Don't take any letters out. Just change the letters around and you can change *liar* into *rail*." For an unusual word like *liar*, give them a meaning they might understand. "The boy did not tell the truth and his friends called him a liar."

is	ads/	lids	rails/	lizard	**lizards**
as	sad	lads	liars		
ad	lad	liar/			
	lid	rail			
		sail			

SORT FOR: l   ad   ail   s (plural)

WRITING AND NEED TO SPELL:

       pad (-ad)

       mail (-ail)

(Perhaps they are writing about writing letters!)

Copyright © 1994, Good Apple

G1498

LETTERS:  a e g m n s t

WORDS TO MAKE:

Give children clues about how many letters to use and how many letters to change. "Now we're going to make some three-letter words. Hold up three fingers! Change just the vowel and you can change the word *man* into *men*." For words like *net/ten* which can be made from the same letters, tell the children, "Don't take any letters out. Just change the letters around and you can change *net* into *ten*." Also, alert the children when they should take all the letters out and start from scratch to make a new word. "Now take all the letters out and start over and make the new four-letter word *mean*." For an unusual word like *mane*, give them a meaning they might understand. "The lion had a beautiful mane around his face."

at	man	mean/	steam	magnet	magnets
an	men	mane			
	met	mate/			
	mat	meat			
	Nat	neat			
	net/	stem			
	ten				
	tan				

SORT FOR: m n at an en et eat e (ea)

WRITING AND NEED TO SPELL:

pet (-et)

treat (-eat)

(Perhaps they are writing about what their pets like!)

Copyright © 1994, Good Apple

G1498

LETTERS: 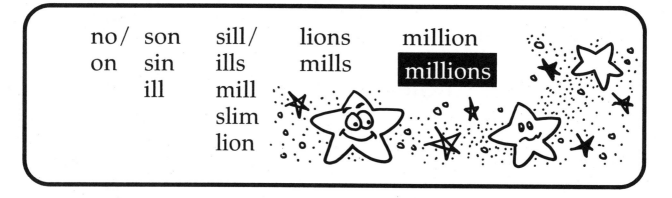 i i o l l m n s

WORDS TO MAKE:

Give children clues about how many letters to use and how many letters to change. "Now we're going to make some three-letter words. Hold up three fingers! Change just the vowel and you can change the word *son* into the word *sin*." For words like *sill/ills* which can be made from the same letters, tell the children, "Don't take any letters out. Just change the letters around and you can change *sill* into *ills*." Also, alert the children when they should take all the letters out and start from scratch to make a new word. "Now take all the letters out and start over and make the word *slim*." For an unusual word like *million*, give them a meaning they might understand. "Some people say there are a million stars in the sky."

no/	son	sill/	lions	million
on	sin	ills	mills	millions
	ill	mill		
		slim		
		lion		

SORT FOR: m   s   ill   s (plural)

WRITING AND NEED TO SPELL:

      spill (-ill)

      spills (-s plural)

(Perhaps they are writing about things that make big messes!)

Copyright © 1994, Good Apple

G1498

LETTERS:  e o k m n s y

WORDS TO MAKE:

Give children clues about how many letters to use and how many letters to change. "Now we're going to make some four-letter words. Hold up four fingers!" Alert the children when they should take all the letters out and start from scratch to make a new word. "Now take all the letters out and start over and make the five-letter word *smoke*." For an unusual word like *monk*, give them a meaning they might understand. "The monk lived a quiet life and spent most of his time praying."

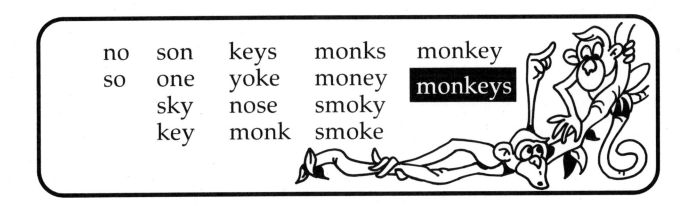

no	son	keys	monks	monkey
so	one	yoke	money	monkeys
	sky	nose	smoky	
	key	monk	smoke	

SORT FOR: s   m   sm   oke

WRITING AND NEED TO SPELL:

joke (-oke)

jokes (-s)

(Perhaps they are writing a joke book!)

Copyright © 1994, Good Apple

G1498

LETTERS:  e o m n r s t

WORDS TO MAKE:

Give children clues about how many letters to use and how many letters to change. "Now we're going to make some three-letter words. Hold up three fingers! Change just the first letter and you can change the word *rot* into *not*." For words like *not/ton* which can be made from the same letters, tell the children, "Don't take any letters out. Just change the letters around and you can change *not* into *ton*." Also, alert the children when they should take all the letters out and start from scratch to make a new word. "Now take all the letters out and start over and make the four-letter word *most*."

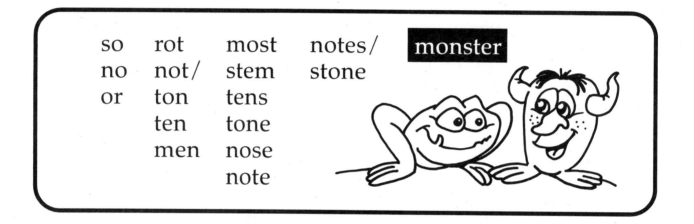

so	rot	most	notes/	monster
no	not/	stem	stone	
or	ton	tens		
	ten	tone		
	men	nose		
		note		

SORT FOR: m   n   t   en   one   ot

WRITING AND NEED TO SPELL:

     Spot (-ot)

     bone (-one)

(Perhaps they are writing about a famous dog!)

Copyright © 1994, Good Apple

G1498

LETTERS:  i o g m n n r

WORDS TO MAKE:

Give children clues about how many letters to use and how many letters to change. "Now we're going to make some four-letter words. Hold up four fingers! Change just the last letter and you can change the word *grin* into *grim*." For words like *ring/grin* which can be made from the same letters, tell the children, "Don't take any letters out. Just change the letters around and you can change *ring* into *grin*." Also, alert the children when they should take all the letters out and start from scratch to make a new word. "Now take all the letters out and start over and make the four-letter word *iron*." For an unusual word like *minor*, give them a meaning they might understand. "It was a minor problem and could be solved quickly."

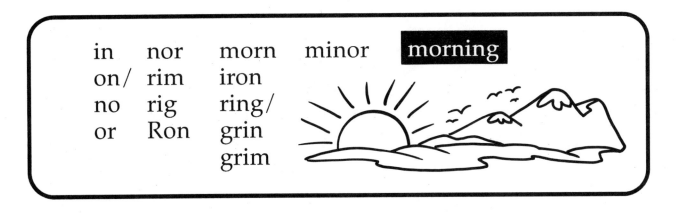

in	nor	morn	minor	**morning**
on/	rim	iron		
no	rig	ring/		
or	Ron	grin		
		grim		

SORT FOR: m   r   gr   in   im

WRITING AND NEED TO SPELL:

Jim (-im)

slim (-im)

(Perhaps they are writing about a skinny friend or a spicy treat!)

WORDS TO MAKE:

Give children clues about how many letters to use and how many letters to change. "Now we're going to make some four-letter words. Hold up four fingers! Change just the first letter and you can change the word *tore* into *more*." For words like *thermos/smother/mothers* which can be made from the same letters, tell the children, "Don't take any letters out. Just change the letters around and you can change *thermos* into *smother* then *mothers*." Also, alert the children when they should take all the letters out and start from scratch to make a new word. "Now take all the letters out and start over and make the five-letter word *store*." For an unusual word like *moth*, give them a meaning they might understand. "The moth they found looked like a butterfly but not so big or pretty." Give them meanings for the homophones *or* and *ore* as you ask them to make those words.

or	toe	tore	moths	others	thermos/
to	ore	more	those	mother	smother/
		most	store		**mothers**
		moth	other		

SORT FOR: m t ore other
or-ore (homophones)

WRITING AND NEED TO SPELL:
bore (-ore)
brother (-other)

(Perhaps they are writing about taking care of a little brother!)

Copyright © 1994, Good Apple

G1498

LETTERS:  a i o u m n n t

WORDS TO MAKE:

Give children clues about how many letters to use and how many letters to change. "Now we're going to make some three-letter words. Hold up three fingers! Change just the last letter and you can change the word *man* into *mat*." For words like *mat/tam* which can be made from the same letters, tell the children, "Don't take any letters out. Just change the letters around and you can change *mat* into *tam*." Also, alert the children when they should take all the letters out and start over and make the word *atom*. For an unusual word like *tam*, give them a meaning they might understand. "The girl had a pretty, purple tam on her head."

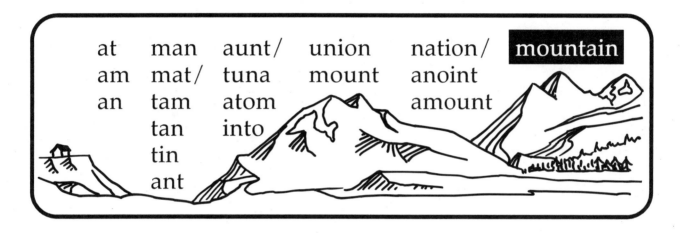

at	man	aunt/	union	nation/	**mountain**
am	mat/	tuna	mount	anoint	
an	tam	atom		amount	
	tan	into			
	tin				
	ant				

SORT FOR: m   t   an   at
into (compound)

WRITING AND NEED TO SPELL:

pan (-an)
flat (-at)

(Perhaps they are writing about making pancakes!)

Copyright © 1994, Good Apple

G1498

LETTERS:  i u f f m n s

WORDS TO MAKE:

Give children clues about how many letters to use and how many letters to change. "Now we're going to make some three-letter words. Hold up three fingers! Change just one letter and you can change the word *fin* into *fun*." Also, alert the children when they should take all the letters out and start from scratch to make a new word. "Now take all the letters out and start over and make the four-letter word *muff*." For an unusual word like *muff*, give them a meaning they might understand. "The girl put her hands into her new muff."

is	fin	fins	muffs	muffin	**muffins**
in	fun	muff	snuff		
	sun		sniff		
	sum		minus		

SORT FOR: m   sn   in   un   uff   s (plural)

WRITING AND NEED TO SPELL:

bin (-in)

stuff (-uff)

(Perhaps they are writing about cleaning up their rooms!)

Copyright © 1994, Good Apple

G1498

LETTERS:  i g h n t s

WORDS TO MAKE:

Give children clues about how many letters to use and how many letters to change. "Now we're going to make some three-letter words. Hold up three fingers! Change just the first letter and you can change the word *hit* into *sit*." For words like *this/hits* which can be made from the same letters, tell the children, "Don't take any letters out. Just change the letters around and you can change *this* into *hits*." Also, alert the children when they should take all the letters out and start from scratch to make a new word. "Now take all the letters out and start over and make the four-letter word *sing*."

is	hit	this/	sight	nights
it	sit	hits	thing	
	his	hint	sting	
		sing/	night	
		sign		
		sigh		

SORT FOR: h s it ing ight

WRITING AND NEED TO SPELL:
bring (-ing)
bright (-ight)

(Perhaps they are writing about birds building their nests!)

LETTERS:  a a e o l m t

WORDS TO MAKE:

Give children clues about how many letters to use and how many letters to change. "Now we're going to make some four-letter words. Hold up four fingers!" For words like *teal*/*tale* which can be made from the same letters, tell the children, "Don't take any letters out. Just change the letters around and you can change *teal* into *tale*." Also, alert the children when they should take all the letters out and start from scratch to make a new word. "Now take all the letters out and start over and make the word *ale*." For an unusual word like *ale*, give them a meaning they might understand. "The man drank ale with his meal."

to	toe	teal/	metal	tamale	oatmeal
	oat	tale	motel		
	ale	male/			
	ate/	meal			
	eat/	meat/			
	tea	team			

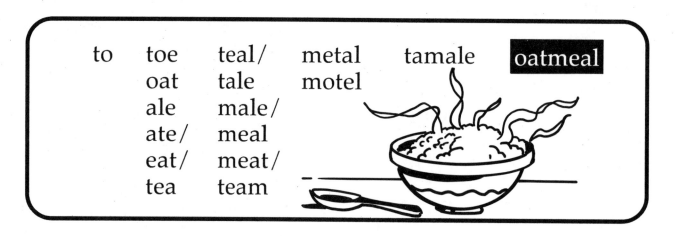

SORT FOR: m t ale eal eat

WRITING AND NEED TO SPELL:

stale (-ale)

wheat (-eat)

(Perhaps they are writing about bread!)

Copyright © 1994, Good Apple

G1498

LETTERS:  a e o g n r s

WORDS TO MAKE:

Give children clues about how many letters to use and how many letters to change. "Now we're going to make some four-letter words. Hold up four fingers! Change just the first letter and you can change the word *sage* into *rage*." For words like *sag/gas* which can be made from the same letters, tell the children, "Don't take any letters out. Just change the letters around and you can change gas into sag." Also, alert the children when they should take all the letters out and start from scratch to make a new word. "Now take all the letters out and start over and make the word *groan*." For an unusual word like *sage*, give them a meaning they might understand. "Cooks use sage to spice up their soups."

as	gas/	sage	range/	reason	oranges
	sag	rage	anger	orange	
	nag	rags	groan/		
	rag		organ		
	age				

SORT FOR: r   ag   age   s (plural)

WRITING AND NEED TO SPELL:

wag (-ag)

cage (-age)

(Perhaps they are writing about taking a pet to the vet!)

Copyright © 1994, Good Apple

LETTERS:  a a e c l p

WORDS TO MAKE:

Give children clues about how many letters to use and how many letters to change. "Now we're going to make some three-letter words. Hold up three fingers! Change just the middle letter and you can change the word *ape* into *ace*." For words like *pal/lap* which can be made from the same letters, tell the children, "Don't take any letters out. Just change the letters around and you can change *pal* into *lap*." For an unusual word like *ace*, give them a meaning they might understand. "When playing cards everyone likes to get an ace."

pa	pal/	peal/	place	palace
	lap	pale/		
	ape	leap		
	ace	lace		
	cap	clap		
	pea	cape/		
		pace		

SORT FOR: p ap ace ape a (cap/cape)

WRITING AND NEED TO SPELL:

Grace (-ace)

grape (-ape)

(Perhaps they are writing about a girl who loves grapes!)

Copyright © 1994, Good Apple

G1498

LETTERS:  a e h n p r t

WORDS TO MAKE:

Give children clues about how many letters to use and how many letters to change. "Now we're going to make some three-letter words. Hold up three fingers! Change just the first letter and you can change the word *hat* into *rat*." For words like *ate/eat* which can be made from the same letters, tell the children, "Don't take any letters out. Just change the letters around and you can change *ate* into *eat*." Also, alert the children when they should take all the letters out and start from scratch to make a new word. "Now take all the letters out and start over and make the four-letter word *path*."

an	hat	heat	parent	panther
at	rat	neat		
	pat	rent		
	pan	path		
	pen			
	pet			
	net			
	ate/			
	eat			

SORT FOR: p   at   et   eat

WRITING AND NEED TO SPELL:

> yet (-et)
>
> seat (-eat)

(Perhaps they are writing about a crowded school bus!)

Copyright © 1994, Good Apple

G1498

LETTERS:  a a e d p r s

WORDS TO MAKE:

Give children clues about how many letters to use and how many letters to change. "Now we're going to make some three-letter words. Hold up three fingers! Change just the first letter and you can change the word *sad* into *pad*." For words like *par/rap* which can be made from the same letters, tell the children, "Don't take any letters out. Just change the letters around and you can change *par* into *rap*." For an unusual word like *par*, give them a meaning they might understand. "Four was par on that hole of the golf course."

as	sad	pear/	drape/	parade	parades
ad	pad	pare	pared		
	par/	read/			
	rap	dear/			
	sap	dare			
	ape/				
	pea				

SORT FOR: p ad ap are ape
pare-pear (homophones)

WRITING AND NEED TO SPELL:
glad (-ad)
map (-ap)

(Perhaps they are writing about a treasure hunt!)

Copyright © 1994, Good Apple

G1498

LETTERS:  a e n p r s t

WORDS TO MAKE:

Give children clues about how many letters to use and how many letters to change. "Now we're going to make some three-letter words. Hold up three fingers! Change just the middle letter and you can change the word *ant* into *art*." For words like *art/rat* which can be made from the same letters, tell the children, "Don't take any letters out. Just change the letters around and you can change *art* into *rat*." For an unusual word like *rant*, give them a meaning they might understand. "Some people rant and rave when they make a mistake."

as	ant	sent	paste	parent	**parents**
at	art/	rent	pants		
	rat	rant			
	pat	pant			
	pet	past			
	net				
	set				

SORT FOR: p   at   et   ant   ent

WRITING AND NEED TO SPELL:

> mat (-at)
>
> tent (-ent)

(Perhaps they are writing about camping out!)

Copyright © 1994, Good Apple

G1498

LETTERS: 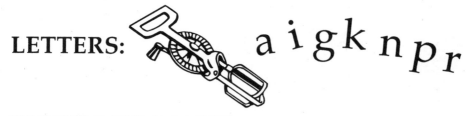 a i g k n p r

WORDS TO MAKE:

Give children clues about how many letters to use and how many letters to change. "Now we're going to make some three-letter words. Hold up three fingers! Change just the first letter and you can change the word *kin* into *pin*." For words like *ink/kin* which can be made from the same letters, tell the children, "Don't take any letters out. Just change the letters around and you can change *ink* into *kin*." Also, alert the children when they should take all the letters out and start from scratch to make a new word. "Now take all the letters out and start over and make the word *grain*." For an unusual word like *nip*, give them a meaning they might understand. "The dog took a nip out of the mail carrier's trousers."

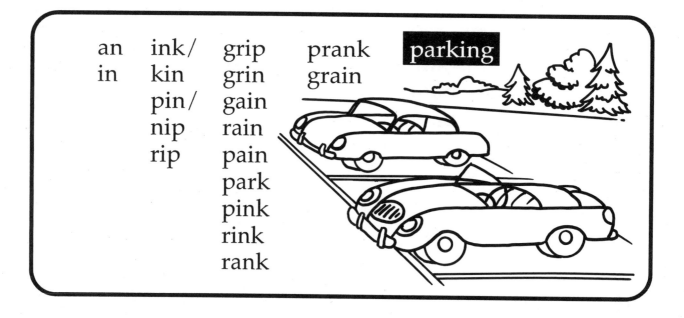

an	ink/	grip	prank	parking
in	kin	grin	grain	
	pin/	gain		
	nip	rain		
	rip	pain		
		park		
		pink		
		rink		
		rank		

SORT FOR: p   r   in   ip   ain   ink

WRITING AND NEED TO SPELL:

train (-ain)

trip (-ip)

(Perhaps they are writing about a train trip!)

Copyright © 1994, Good Apple

G1498

LETTERS:  a o p r r s t

WORDS TO MAKE:

Give children clues about how many letters to use and how many letters to change. "Now we're going to make some three-letter words. Hold up three fingers! Change just the first letter and you can change the word *pat* into *rat*." For words like *pot/top* which can be made from the same letters, tell the children, "Don't take any letters out. Just change the letters around and you can change *pot* into *top*." Also, alert the children when they should take all the letters out and start from scratch to make a new word. "Now take all the letters out and start over and make the word *roar*." For an unusual word like *port*, give them a meaning they might understand. "The cruise ship pulled into port and the passengers got off."

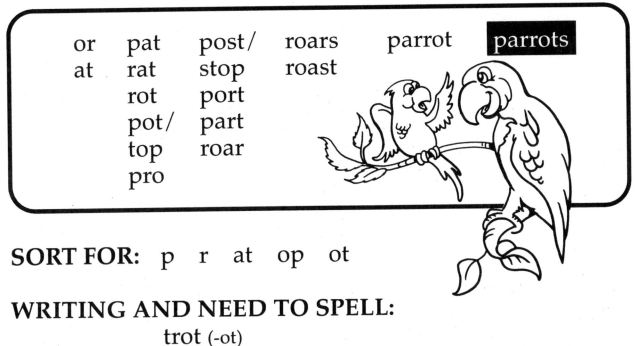

or	pat	post/	roars	parrot	parrots
at	rat	stop	roast		
	rot	port			
	pot/	part			
	top	roar			
	pro				

SORT FOR: p r at op ot

WRITING AND NEED TO SPELL:

trot (-ot)

clop (-op)

(Perhaps they are writing about an old horse!)

Copyright © 1994, Good Apple

G1498

LETTERS:  a e u n p s t

A two-day lesson or pick and choose some words.
You may want to make all words one day and sort/spell the next day.

WORDS TO MAKE:

Give children clues about how many letters to use and how many letters to change. "Now we're going to make some three-letter words. Hold up three fingers! Change just the first letter and you can change the word *tan* into *pan*." For words like *eat/tea* which can be made from the same letters, tell the children, "Don't take any letters out. Just change the letters around and you can change *eat* into *tea*." Also, alert the children when they should take all the letters out and start from scratch to make a new word. "Now take all the letters out and start over and make the five-letter word *upset*."

us	eat/	aunt	paste/	peanut	peanuts
as	tea	pant	tapes		
an	tan	pans	pause		
at	pan	pets/	upset		
	pat/	pest	aunts		
	tap	nest/			
	sat	nets			
	set	neat			
	pet	tape			
	net	east			
	nut				
	ant				

SORT FOR: p n t an at et eat est
s (plural)   upset (compound word)

WRITING AND NEED TO SPELL:

cheat (-eat)

tests (-est-s)

(Perhaps they are writing about a student who didn't study!)

Copyright © 1994, Good Apple

LETTERS:  e e b b l p s

WORDS TO MAKE:

Give children clues about how many letters to use and how many letters to change. "Now we're going to make some three-letter words. Hold up three fingers! Change just the first letter and you can change the word *bee* into *see*." For words like *eels/else* which can be made from the same letters, tell the children, "Don't take any letters out. Just change the letters around and you can change *eels* into *else*." For an unusual word like *eel*, give them a meaning they might understand. "An eel is a fish with a long snakelike body."

be	bee	eels/	beeps	pebble	pebbles
	see	else	sleep/		
	eel	peel	peels		
		seep			
		bees			
		beep			

SORT FOR: b p ee eel eep s (plural)
be-bee (homophones)

WRITING AND NEED TO SPELL:

heel (-eel)

steep (-eep)

(Perhaps they are writing about mountain climbing!)

Copyright © 1994, Good Apple

G1498

LETTERS:  e i c d k p

WORDS TO MAKE:

Give children clues about how many letters to use and how many letters to change. "Now we're going to make some three-letter words. Hold up three fingers! Change just the first letter and you can change the word *pie* into *die*." Alert the children when they should take all the letters out and start from scratch to make a new word. "Now take all the letters out and start over and make the word *iced*." For an unusual word like *epic*, give them a meaning they might understand. "The poem was a long one and the teacher said it was an epic."

kid dice **picked**
dip Dick
pie pick
die pike
ice peck
     deck
     dike
     iced
     epic

SORT FOR: p d ie ice ick eck

WRITING AND NEED TO SPELL:

> price (-ice)
> check (-eck)

(Perhaps they are writing about eating in a restaurant!)

Copyright © 1994, Good Apple

G1498

LETTERS: e i u c p r s t

A two-day lesson or pick and choose some words.
You may want to make all words one day and sort/spell the next day.

WORDS TO MAKE:

Give children clues about how many letters to use and how many letters to change. "Now we're going to make some three-letter words. Hold up three fingers! Change just the first letter and you can change the word *pit* into *sit*." For words like *tires/tries* which can be made from the same letters, tell the children, "Don't take any letters out. Just change the letters around and you can change *tires* into *tries*." Also, alert the children when they should take all the letters out and start from scratch to make a new word. "Now take all the letters out and start over and make the word *pie*." For an unusual word like *pure*, give them a meaning they might understand. "The milk was pure and fresh from a cow."

us	pit	rice	tires/	ripest	picture
up	sit	cuts	tries	prices	pictures
it	set	cute	price	purest	
	pet	pure	purse	uprise	
	put	pies	cries	cruise	
	cut	rise	crisp		
	pie	tire	crust		
	tie	ripe	cuter		
	ice		upset		

SORT FOR: p it et i ice er/est (endings)

WRITING AND NEED TO SPELL:

jet (-et)
die (-ie)

(Perhaps they are writing about a plane crash!)

Copyright © 1994, Good Apple

G1498

LETTERS:  a e l n p s t

WORDS TO MAKE:

Give children clues about how many letters to use and how many letters to change. "Now we're going to make some five-letter words. Hold up five fingers! Change just the first letter and you can change the word *slate* into *plate*." For words like *pale/peal* which can be made from the same letters, tell the children, "Don't take any letters out. Just change the letters around and you can change *pale* into *peal*." Also, alert the children when they should take all the letters out and start from scratch to make a new word. "Now take all the letters out and start over and make the four-letter word *slat*." For an unusual word like *slat*, give them a meaning they might understand. "The slat fell down from under the bed."

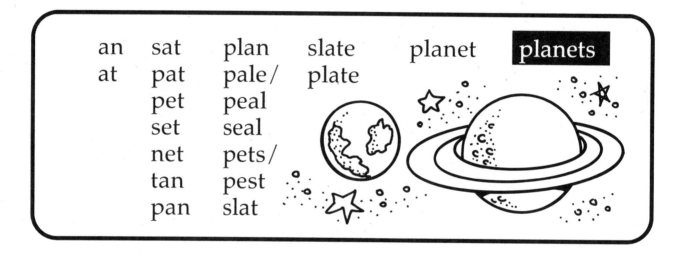

an	sat	plan	slate	planet	**planets**
at	pat	pale/	plate		
	pet	peal			
	set	seal			
	net	pets/			
	tan	pest			
	pan	slat			

SORT FOR: p pl at et an ate eal

WRITING AND NEED TO SPELL:

meal (-eal)

skate (-ate)

(Perhaps they are writing about a party at the skating rink!)

Copyright © 1994, Good Apple

G1498

LETTERS:  a e l n p p y

WORDS TO MAKE:

Give children clues about how many letters to use and how many letters to change. "Now we're going to make some four-letter words. Hold up four fingers! Change just the last letter and you can change the word *play* into *plan*." For words like *pal/lap* which can be made from the same letters, tell the children, "Don't take any letters out. Just change the letters around and you can change *pal* into *lap*." Also, alert the children when they should take all the letters out and start from scratch to make a new word. "Now take all the letters out and start over and make the five-letter word *apple*." For an unusual word like *apply*, give them a meaning they might understand. "The teenager went to McDonald's to apply for a job."

an	pan	play	plane/	playpen
	pen	leap	panel	
	pal/	lean	apple	
	lap	plan	apply	
	nap			
	lay			
	pay/			
	yap			

SORT FOR: p l pl an ap ay

WRITING AND NEED TO SPELL:

trap (-ap)

away (-ay)

(Perhaps they are writing about an animal caught in a trap!)

Copyright © 1994, Good Apple

G1498

LETTERS:  e o c k p s t

WORDS TO MAKE:

Give children clues about how many letters to use and how many letters to change. "Now we're going to make some six-letter words. Hold up six fingers! Change just the first letter and you can change the word *socket* into *pocket*." For words like *pots/post/spot/stop* which can be made from the same letters, tell the children, "Don't take any letters out. Just change the letters around and you can change *pots* into *post*, *spot* and *stop*." Also, alert the children when they should take all the letters out and start from scratch to make a new word. "Now take all the letters out and start over and make the word *poke*."

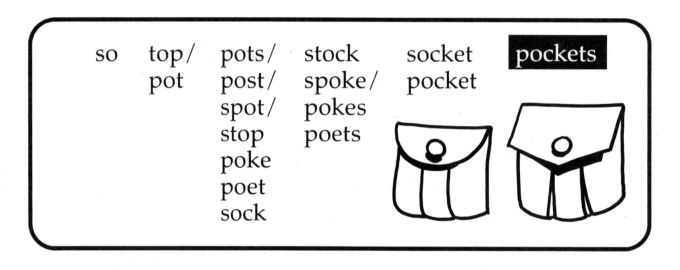

so	top/	pots/	stock	socket	pockets
	pot	post/	spoke/	pocket	
		spot/	pokes		
		stop	poets		
		poke			
		poet			
		sock			

SORT FOR: p s sp st op ot ock

WRITING AND NEED TO SPELL:
    clock (-ock)
    shop (-op)

(Perhaps they are writing about going shopping!)

Copyright © 1994, Good Apple

G1498

LETTERS:  a e o o p t t s

WORDS TO MAKE:

Give children clues about how many letters to use and how many letters to change. "Now we're going to make some five-letter words. Hold up five fingers! Change just the first letter and you can change the word *paste* into the word *taste*." For words like *pots/post* which can be made from the same letters, tell the children, "Don't take any letters out. Just change the letters around and you can change *pots* into *post*." Also, alert the children when they should take all the letters out and start from scratch to make a new word. "Now take all the letters out and start over and make the six-letter word *potato*."

to	sat	toes	poets	potato	teapots
at	pat	pots/	paste	teapot	**potatoes**
	pot	post	taste		
	tot	poet			
	toe				

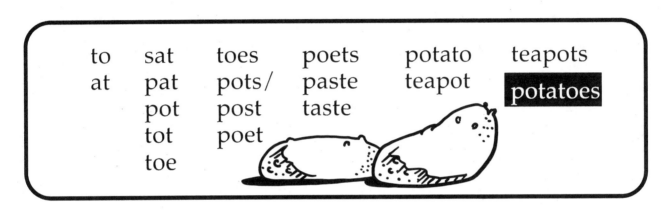

SORT FOR: p t at ot aste s/es (plural)

WRITING AND NEED TO SPELL:

> waste (-aste)
>
> slot (-ot)

(Perhaps they are writing about recycling!)

Copyright © 1994, Good Apple

WORDS TO MAKE:

Give children clues about how many letters to use and how many letters to change. "Now we're going to make some three-letter words. Hold up three fingers! Change just the last letter and you can change the word *pen* into the word *pet*." For words like *pets/step* which can be made from the same letters, tell the children, "Don't take any letters out. Just change the letters around and you can change *pets* into *step*." Also, alert the children when they should take all the letters out and start over and make the five-letter word *reset*." For an unusual word like *repent*, give them a meaning they might understand. "The preacher told the sinner to repent."

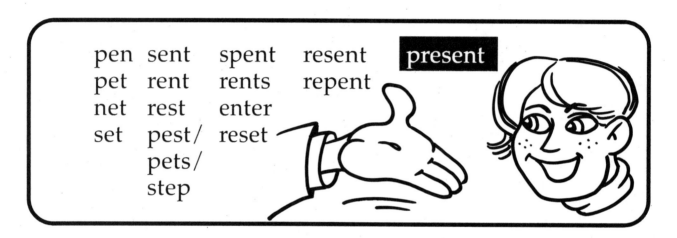

pen	sent	spent	resent	**present**
pet	rent	rents	repent	
net	rest	enter		
set	pest/	reset		
	pets/			
	step			

SORT FOR: p   et   ent   est   re (prefix)

WRITING AND NEED TO SPELL:

jet (-et)

went (-ent)

(Perhaps they are writing about a trip they went on!)

Copyright © 1994, Good Apple

G1498

LETTERS:  e i c n p r s s

A two-day lesson or pick and choose some words.
You may want to make all words one day and sort/spell the next day.

WORDS TO MAKE:

Give children clues about how many letters to use and how many letters to change. "Now we're going to make some three-letter words. Hold up three fingers! Change just the vowel and you can change the word *pin* into *pen*." Also alert the children when they should take all the letters out and start from scratch to make a new word. "Now take all the letters out and start over and make the word *spin*." For words like *spin/pins* which can be made from the same letters, tell the children, "Don't take any letters out. Just change the letters around and you can change *spin* to *pins*."

is	pin	ripe	risen	spices	princes
in	pen	rice	ripen	prices	**princess**
	pie	nice	price	prince	
	ice	spin/	spice		
	rip	pins	spine		
		pens	since		
		pine			
		rise			

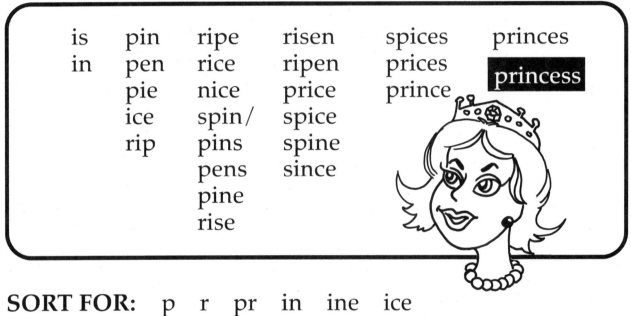

SORT FOR: p   r   pr   in   ine   ice
s (plural)   en (risen, ripen)

WRITING AND NEED TO SPELL:

twins (-in, -s)

twice (-ice)

(Perhaps they are writing about how twins need two of everything!)

Copyright © 1994, Good Apple

G1498

LETTERS:  e o b l m p r s

WORDS TO MAKE:

Give children clues about how many letters to use and how many letters to change. "Now we're going to make some three-letter words. Hold up three fingers! Change just the last letter and you can change the word *mop* into *mob*." Alert the children when they should take all the letters out and start from scratch to make a new word. "Now take all the letters out and start over and make the six-letter word *morsel*." For an unusual word like *probe*, give them a meaning they might understand. "The spaceship will probe outer space."

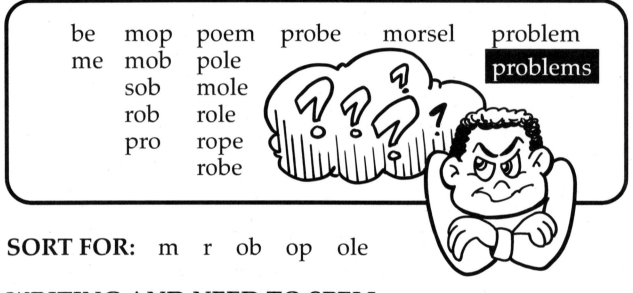

be	mop	poem	probe	morsel	problem
me	mob	pole			problems
	sob	mole			
	rob	role			
	pro	rope			
		robe			

SORT FOR: m r ob op ole

WRITING AND NEED TO SPELL:

job (-ob)

crop (-op)

(Perhaps they are writing about a summer of working on a farm!)

Copyright © 1994, Good Apple
G1498

WORDS TO MAKE:

Give children clues about how many letters to use and how many letters to change. "Now we're going to make some four-letter words. Hold up four fingers! Change just the last letter and you can change the word *skip* into *skin*." For words like *skin/sink* which can be made from the same letters, tell the children, "Don't take any letters out. Just change the letters around and you can change *skin* into *sink*." Also, alert the children when they should take all the letters out and start from scratch to make a new word. "Now take all the letters out and start over and make the word *mink*." For an unusual word like *spunk*, give them a meaning they might understand. "The actor had a lot of spunk and was not afraid to do his own stunts."

us	ink/	skip	spunk	pumpkin
in	kin	skin/	minus	**pumpkins**
	ski	sink		
		spin		
		mink		
		pink		
		punk		
		pump		

SORT FOR: p sk sp in ink unk

WRITING AND NEED TO SPELL:

stink (-ink)

skunk (-unk)

(Perhaps they are writing about skunks!)

Copyright © 1994, Good Apple
G1498

LETTERS:  e i u p p p s

WORDS TO MAKE:

Give children clues about how many letters to use and how many letters to change. "Now we're going to make some two-letter words. Hold up two fingers! Change just the last letter and you can change the word *us* into *up*." For words like *use/Sue* which can be made from the same letters, tell the children, "Don't take any letters out. Just change the letters around and you can change *use* into *Sue*." Remind them to turn their letters over for the capital letter to begin a name. Also, alert the children when they should take all the letters out and start from scratch to make a new word. "Now take all the letters out and start over and make the word *sip*." For an unusual word like *pep*, give them a meaning they might understand. "The cheerleaders had lots of pep during the football game."

is	pup	pies	pipes	puppies
us	sup	pipe		
up	use/	pups		
	Sue			
	sip			
	pep			
	pie			

SORT FOR: p   up   s/es (plural)

WRITING AND NEED TO SPELL:

cup (-up)

cups (-plural)

(Perhaps they are writing about baking!)

Copyright © 1994, Good Apple

G1498

LETTERS:  eudhps

WORDS TO MAKE:

Give children clues about how many letters to use and how many letters to change. "Now we're going to make some three-letter words. Hold up three fingers!" For words like *use/Sue* which can be made from the same letters, tell the children, "Don't take any letters out. Just change the letters around and you can change *use* into *Sue*." Remind the children to turn the lowercase letter over for the capital letter when they make a name. Give clues on how many letters to change, "Change just one letter and you can change the word *Sue* into *due*." Also, alert the children when they should take all the letters out and start from scratch to make a new word. "Now take all the letters out and start over and make the word *push*." For an unusual word like *spud*, give them a meaning they might understand. "The boy called his potato a spud."

Ed	use/	dues/	**pushed**
up	Sue	used	
us	she	push	
	due	spud	
		sped	
		shed	

SORT FOR: sh sp ed ue

WRITING AND NEED TO SPELL:
> red (-ed)
>
> blue (-ue)

(Perhaps they are writing about the American flag or favorite colors!)

Copyright © 1994, Good Apple

G1498

LETTERS:  a i u c g k q n

WORDS TO MAKE:

Give children clues about how many letters to use and how many letters to change. "Now we're going to make some three-letter words. Hold up three fingers! Add one letter to the word *in* and you have the three-letter word *ink*." For words like *ink/kin* which can be made from the same letters, tell the children, "Don't take any letters out. Just change the letters around and you can change *ink* into *kin*." Alert the children when they should take all the letters out and start from scratch to make a new word. "Now take all the letters out and start over and make the word *gain*." For an unusual word like *gunk*, give them a meaning they might understand. "The can of oil was so dirty the man called it gunk."

an	ink/	gunk	quick	quaking
in	kin	gain	quack	quacking
	can	nick		
	nag	king		
	gun			

SORT FOR: qu g ick

WRITING AND NEED TO SPELL:
> stick (-ick)
>
> kick (-ick)

(Perhaps they are writing about hockey!)

Copyright © 1994, Good Apple

G1498

LETTERS:  a e u q r r s t

WORDS TO MAKE:

Give children clues about how many letters to use and how many letters to change. "Now we're going to make some three-letter words. Hold up three fingers! Add one letter to the word *at* and you have the three-letter word *sat*." Also, give clues on what letters to change, "Change just the first letter and you can change *sat* to *rat*." For words like *rat/art* which can be made from the same letters, tell the children, "Don't take any letters out. Just change the letters around and you can change *rat* into *art*." Alert the children when they should take all the letters out and start from scratch to make a new word. "Now take all the letters out and start over and make the word *squat*." For an unusual word like *quest*, give them a meaning they might understand. "The knight and his followers set out on a quest."

as	sat	ruts/	quest	quarts	**quarters**
at	rat/	rust	squat	square	
	art	rest	quart	quarter	
	rut				

SORT FOR: qu squ r est at s (plural)

WRITING AND NEED TO SPELL:

pest (-est)

brat (-at)

(Perhaps they are writing about a little cousin!)

Copyright © 1994, Good Apple

G1498

WORDS TO MAKE:

Give children clues about how many letters to use and how many letters to change. "Now we're going to make some three-letter words." Also, give clues on what letters to change, "Change just the first letter and you can change *rat* to *sat*." For words like *art/rat* which can be made from the same letters, tell the children, "Don't take any letters out. Just change the letters around and you can change *art* into *rat*." Alert the children when they should take all the letters out and start from scratch to make a new word. "Now take all the letters out and start over and make the word *sir*." For an unusual word like *rabbi*, give them a meaning they might understand. "The Jewish rabbi led the ceremony at the temple."

at	air	stir	stair	rabbit
as	art/	star	rabbi	rabbits
	rat			
	sat			
	bat			
	bar			
	tar			
	sir			

SORT FOR: r   st   at   ar

WRITING AND NEED TO SPELL:

car (-ar)

flat (-at)

(Perhaps they are writing about getting a flat tire!)

Copyright © 1994, Good Apple

G1498

LETTERS:  a i g k n r

WORDS TO MAKE:

Give children clues about how many letters to use and how many letters to change. "Now we're going to make some three-letter words. Add one letter to the word *in* and you have the three-letter word *kin*." Alert the children when they should take all the letters out and start from scratch to make a new word. "Now take all the letters out and start over and make the word *ran*." Also, give clues on what letters to change, "Change just the first letter and you can change *nag* to *rag*." For an unusual word like *rig*, give them a meaning they might understand. "They will rig the car with a stereo system."

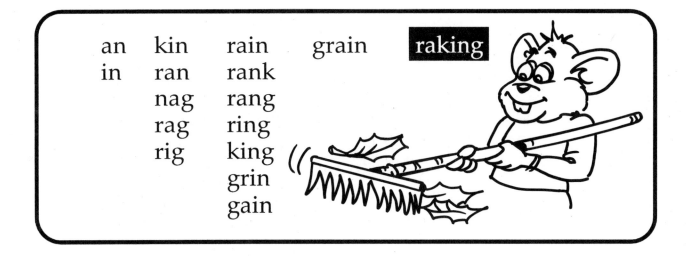

an	kin	rain	grain	raking
in	ran	rank		
	nag	rang		
	rag	ring		
	rig	king		
		grin		
		gain		

SORT FOR: r   ain   in   ing

WRITING AND NEED TO SPELL:

sprain (-ain)

sling (-ing)

(Perhaps they are writing about an accident and a sore arm!)

Copyright © 1994, Good Apple

G1498

LETTERS:  e e e i d n r r

WORDS TO MAKE:

Give children clues about how many letters to use and how many letters to change. "Now we're going to make some five-letter words. Add one letter to the four-letter word *ride* and you have the five-letter word *rider*." Also, give clues on what letters to change, "Change just the first letter and you can change *reed* to *need*." For words like *deer/reed* which can be made from the same letters, tell the children, "Don't take any letters out. Just change the letters around and you can change *deer* into *reed*." Alert the children when they should take all the letters out and start from scratch to make a new word. "Now take all the letters out and start over and make the word *rein*." For an unusual word like *rein* or *reed*, give them a meaning they might understand. "The girl pulled on the rein to stop the horse. This reed is a piece of hard grass."

in red   dine   rider/   **reindeer**
rid   deer/   drier
die   reed   diner
     need
     rein
     rind
     ride

SORT FOR: r d eed er (ending)

WRITING AND NEED TO SPELL:

feed (-eed)

feeder (-er ending)

(Perhaps they are writing about birds!)

Copyright © 1994, Good Apple

G1498

LETTERS:  e o o r r s s t

WORDS TO MAKE:

Give children clues about how many letters to use and how many letters to change. "Now we're going to make some four-letter words. Add one letter to the word *ore* and you have the four-letter word *sore*." Also, give clues on what letters to change, "Change just the first letter and you can change *sore* to *tore*." For words like *tore/rote* which can be made from the same letters, tell the children, "Don't take any letters out. Just change the letters around and you can change *tore* into *rote*." For an unusual word like *rote*, give them a meaning they might understand. "Most children can say the alphabet by rote."

so	rot	sore	roots/	stores	rooster
to	ore	tore/	roost	rooter	**roosters**
		rote	store		
		rose			
		root			

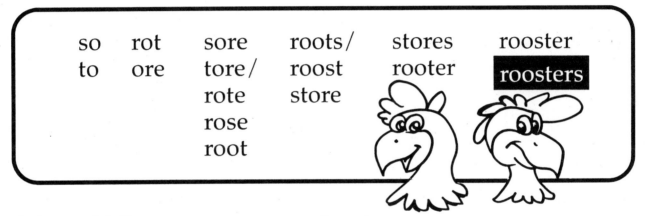

SORT FOR: r t ore s-plural

WRITING AND NEED TO SPELL:

shore (-ore)

shores (-s)

(Perhaps they are writing about the beach!)

Copyright © 1994, Good Apple

G1498

LETTERS:  a a i o b l s t

A two-day lesson or pick and choose some words.
You may want to make all words one day and sort/spell the next day.

WORDS TO MAKE:

Give children clues about how many letters to use and how many letters to change.
"Now we're going to make some three-letter words. Add one letter to the word *it* and
you have the three-letter word *bit*." Also, give clues on what letters to change, "Change
just the vowel and you can change *sat* to *sit*." For words like *bat/tab* which can be made
from the same letters, tell the children, "Don't take any letters out. Just change the
letters around and you can change *bat* into *tab*." Alert the children when they should
take all the letters out and start over and make the word *lot*. For an unusual word like
slab, give them a meaning they might understand. "The woman chose a *slab* of bacon to
cook for breakfast." Remind the children that *sailboat* is a compound word made from
two words they have already made in this lesson—*sail* and *boat*.

at	bit	lots/	blot	basal	bloats
as	sit	lost/	boat	blast	sailboat
is	sat	slot	boil	boast/	
it	bat/	slit/	toil	boats	
	tab	list	soil	bloat	
	lot	slat/	sail		
		salt/	tail		
		last	bail		
		stab	bait		
		slab			
		slob			

SORT FOR: s sl b bl ab at it ot ail oil
sailboat (compound)

WRITING AND NEED TO SPELL:
snail (-ail)

spoil (-oil)

(Perhaps they are writing about garden pests!)

Copyright © 1994, Good Apple

G1498

LETTERS:  a i c d h n s w

WORDS TO MAKE:

Give children clues about how many letters to use and how many letters to change. "Now we're going to make some three-letter words. Add one letter to the word *ad* and you have the three-letter word *had*." Also, give clues on what letters to change, "Change just the first letter and you can change *had* to *sad*." For words like *saw/was* which can be made from the same letters, tell the children, "Don't take any letters out. Just change the letters around and you can change *saw* into *was*." For an unusual word like *ash*, give them a meaning they might understand. "We sat in the shade of the ash tree to cool off."

ad	had	hand	**sandwich**
	sad	sand	
	saw /	dash	
	was	disc	
	has /	dish	
	ash	wish	
	and		

SORT FOR: s   h   ad   and   ish

WRITING AND NEED TO SPELL:

stand (-and)

squish (-ish)

(Perhaps they are writing about walking in a pond!)

Copyright © 1994, Good Apple

G1498

LETTERS:  a a u d r s t y

A two-day lesson or pick and choose some words.
You may want to make all words one day and sort/spell the next day.

WORDS TO MAKE:

Give children clues about how many letters to use and how many letters to change. "Now we're going to make some four-letter words. Add one letter to the word *try* and you have the four-letter word *tray*." Also, give clues on what letters to change, "Change just the first two letters and you can change *tray* to *stay*." For words like *star/arts* which can be made from the same letters, tell the children, "Don't take any letters out. Just change the letters around and you can change *star* into *arts*." For an unusual word like *arty*, give them a meaning they might understand. "The printer was said to be very arty." Remind the children to turn their letter cards over when they want to make a word like *Saturday* that needs a capital letter.

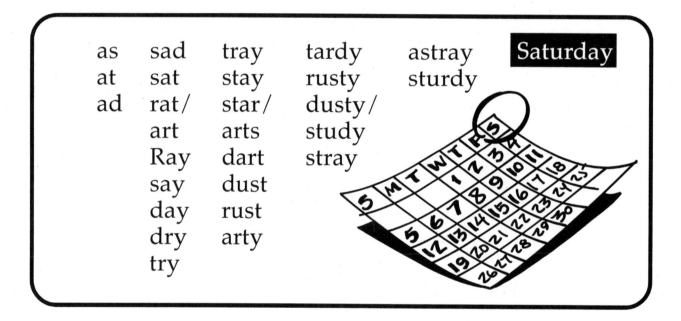

as	sad	tray	tardy	astray	**Saturday**
at	sat	stay	rusty	sturdy	
ad	rat/	star/	dusty/		
	art	arts	study		
	Ray	dart	stray		
	say	dust			
	day	rust			
	dry	arty			
	try				

SORT FOR: s   st   tr   at   ay   ust   y (try, rusty)

WRITING AND NEED TO SPELL:

>   crust (-ust)
>
>   crusty (-y)

(Perhaps they are writing about pizza!)

Copyright © 1994, Good Apple

G1498

LETTERS:  a e c d r s

WORDS TO MAKE:

Give children clues about how many letters to use and how many letters to change. "Now we're going to make some four-letter words. Add just one letter and you can change *car* to *scar*." Alert the children when they should take all the letters out and start from scratch to make a new word. "Now take all the letters out and start over and make the word *are*." For words like *are/ear* which can be made from the same letters, tell the children, "Don't take any letters out. Just change the letters around and you can change *are* into *ear*."

as   sea   scar   cared/   **scared**
       sad   card   raced
       are/   care/   scare
       ear   race
       car   dear/
              read/
              dare

SORT FOR: s   c   sc   ar   are   ear
ed (ending)

(Point out that *are* is not pronounced like all the other *a-r-e* words.)

WRITING AND NEED TO SPELL:
dared (-ed)
fear (-ear)

(Perhaps they are writing about skydiving!)

Copyright © 1994, Good Apple

G1498

LETTERS:  a e e c d h r s

A two-day lesson or pick and choose some words.
You may want to make all words one day and sort/spell the next day.

WORDS TO MAKE:

Give children clues about how many letters to use and how many letters to change. "Now we're going to make some three-letter words. Add one letter to the word *he* and you have the three-letter word *her*." Also, give clues on what letters to change. "Change just the first letter and you can change *sad* to *had*." Alert the children when they should take all the letters out and start from scratch to make a new word. "Now take all but one letter out and make the word *sad*." For words like *are/ear* which can be made from the same letters, tell the children, "Don't take any letters out. Just change the letters around and you can change *are* into *ear*." For an unusual word like *arch*, give them a meaning they might understand. "The golden arch is the symbol for McDonald's." Remember to give meanings for the homophones as you ask the children to make those words.

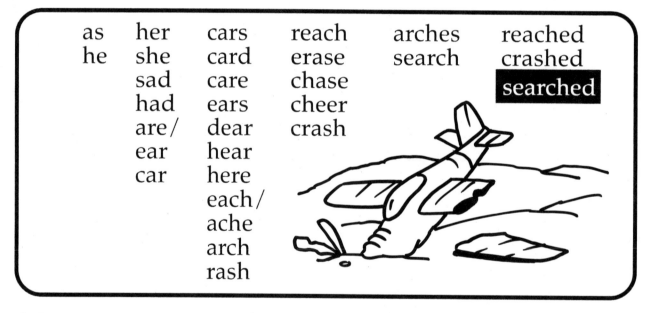

as	her	cars	reach	arches	reached
he	she	card	erase	search	crashed
	sad	care	chase		**searched**
	had	ears	cheer		
	are/	dear	crash		
	ear	hear			
	car	here			
		each/			
		ache			
		arch			
		rash			

SORT FOR: c h ch ad ear s/es (plural)
ed (ending) hear-here (homophones)

(Sort *ache* with the *ch* words and then help children to notice that usually *ch* has the sound in *cheer*, but sometimes it has the sound in *ache*.)

WRITING AND NEED TO SPELL:

spear (-ear)

speared (-ed)

(Perhaps they are writing about catching fish in a stream!)

Copyright © 1994, Good Apple

G1498

LETTERS: a e e h l l s s

WORDS TO MAKE:

Give children clues about how many letters to use and how many letters to change. "Now we're going to make some four-letter words. Make the four-letter word *sell*." Also, give clues on what letters to change, "Change just one letter and you can change *sell* to *seal*." For words like *seal/sale* which can be made from the same letters, tell the children, "Don't take any letters out. Just change the letters around and you can change *seal* into *sale*." Alert the children when they should take all the letters out and start from scratch to make a new word. "Now take all but one letter out and make the word *heal*." For an unusual word like *leash*, give them a meaning they might understand. "The dog was put on a leash when the family walked him." Remember to give meanings for the homophones as you ask the children to make these words. Also, explain that *seashell* is a compound word made from two smaller words they have already made in this lesson–*sea* and *shell*.

he	she	sell	shell	easels	leashes
	sea	seal/	leash	shells	**seashell**
	see	sale	easel		
		heal			
		heel			

SORT FOR: s   sh   ell   s/es (plural)
seashell (compound word)
sea-see, heal-heel (homophones)

WRITING AND NEED TO SPELL:
spell (-ell)
spells (-s plural)
(Perhaps they are writing about a spelling bee!)

Copyright © 1994, Good Apple

LETTERS:  a o d h s w

WORDS TO MAKE:

Give children clues about how many letters to use and how many letters to change. "Now we're going to make some four-letter words. Make the four-letter word *wash*." Also, give clues on what letters to change, "Change just the first letter and you can change *wash* to *dash*." For words like *was/saw* which can be made from the same letters, tell the children, "Don't take any letters out. Just change the letters around and you can change *was* into *saw*." Alert the children when they should take all the letters out and start from scratch to make a new word. "Now take all the letters out and start from scratch to make the word *soda*." For an unusual word like *ad*, give them a meaning they might understand. "The ad on television said that a new toy could be found in my favorite cereal."

do	ads	wash	**shadow**
ho	ash/	dash	
so	has	soda	
as	had	show	
ad	sad		
	was/		
	saw		
	who		

SORT FOR: s sh ad ash

(Point out to the children that *wash* is not pronounced like most a-s-h words.)

WRITING AND NEED TO SPELL:

> mad (-ad)
>
> splash (-ash)

(Perhaps they are writing about splashing someone who didn't want to get splashed!)

Copyright © 1994, Good Apple

G1498

LETTERS:  a b k l s y

WORDS TO MAKE:

Give children clues about how many letters to use and how many letters to change. "Now we're going to make some four-letter words. Add a letter to *sly* and you can make *slay*." Give clues on what letters to change, "Change just the first letter and you can change *say* to *lay*." Alert the children when they should take all the letters out and start from scratch to make a new word. "Now take all but one letter out and make the word *ask*." For words like *slay/lays* which can be made from the same letters, tell the children, "Don't take any letters out. Just change the letters around and you can change *slay* into *lays*." For an unusual word like *balk*, give them a meaning they might understand. "Did the team balk at their chance to play the game over?" Remember to tell the children as you sort that *y* at the end of a word can have two sounds and sort for those sounds. Also, explain that *skylab* is a compound word made up of two smaller words they have already made in this lesson–*sky* and *lab*.

Al	say	slay/	balks	skylab
as	lay	lays	balky	
	lab	labs		
	ask	balk		
	sky			
	sly			

SORT FOR: ay   s (pairs)   y (sky-balky)

WRITING AND NEED TO SPELL:

      pay (-ay)

      pays (-s)

(Perhaps they are writing about making money!)

Copyright © 1994, Good Apple

G1498

LETTERS:  e e i g l n p s

WORDS TO MAKE:

Give children clues about how many letters to use and how many letters to change. "Now we're going to make some four-letter words. Add a letter to *pig* and you can make the plural, *pigs*." Also, give clues on what letters to change, "Change just the first letter and you can change *ping* to *sing*." For an unusual word like *sling*, give them a meaning they might understand. "The boy rested his broken arm in a sling."

is	pin	pigs	sling	seeing	sleeping
in	pig	ping	sleep	seeping	
		sing		peeling	
		spin			
		seep			
		peel			

SORT FOR: p s sl in ing eep
ing (ending)

WRITING AND NEED TO SPELL:

swing (-ing)

swinging (-ing ending)

(Perhaps they are writing about riding on swings on the playground!)

Copyright © 1994, Good Apple

130

G1498

WORDS TO MAKE:

Give children clues about how many letters to use and how many letters to change. "Now we're going to make some three-letter words. Add a letter to *at* and you can make *mat*." Also, give clues on what letters to change, "Change just the first letter and you can change *mat* to *sat*. Change the vowel in *sat* and you can make the word *set*." Alert the children when they should take all the letters out and start from scratch to make a new word. "Now take all but one letter out and make the word *all*." For an unusual word like *stall*, give them a meaning they might understand. "The horse was in his stall."

as	mat	mall	smell	smells	smallest
at	sat	sell	small		
	set	tell	stall		
	met		stale		
	let				
	all				

SORT FOR: s m sm at et all ell

WRITING AND NEED TO SPELL:
> well (-ell)
>
> swell (-ell)

(Perhaps they are writing about getting better after having had poison ivy!)

Copyright © 1994, Good Apple

G1498

LETTERS:  i i f f g n n s

WORDS TO MAKE:

Give children clues about how many letters to use and how many letters to change. "Now we're going to make some three-letter words. Add a letter to *in* and you can make *inn*, a place where you can spend a night away from home." Also, give clues on what letters to change. "Change just one letter and you can change *sin* to *fin*." For words like *sing/sign* which can be made from the same letters, tell the children, "Don't take any letters out. Just change the letters around and you can change *sing* into *sign*." Alert the children when they should take all the letters out and start from scratch to make a new word. "Now take all but one letter out and make the word *inns*."

is	inn	figs	sniff	sniffing
if	sin	fins		
in	fin	sing/		
	fig	sign		
		inns		

SORT FOR: s sn in s (plural)
in-inn (homophones)

WRITING AND NEED TO SPELL:
spin (-in)
spins (-s)

(Perhaps they are writing about a ride at the fair or amusement park!)

Copyright © 1994, Good Apple

132

G1498

LETTERS:  e i d p r s s

WORDS TO MAKE:

Give children clues about how many letters to use and how many letters to change. "Now we're going to make some four-letter words. Add a letter to *dip* and you can make *drip*." Also, give clues on what letters to change, "Change just one letter and you can change *ripe* to *rise*." Remember to tell the children to turn their cards over for the capital they need to begin a name. Alert the children when they should take all the letters out and start from scratch to make a new word. "Now take all but one letter out and make the word *pier*." For an unusual word like *pier*, give them a meaning they might understand. "The people sat on the pier and fished."

is	sip	drip	pride	spider
	Sid	ripe	spied	spiders
	sir	rise		
	rip	ride		
	pie	side		
	dip	pier		

SORT FOR: s p sp ip ide

WRITING AND NEED TO SPELL:
skip (-ip)

slide (-ide)

(Perhaps they are writing about playing on the playground!)

Copyright © 1994, Good Apple

G1498

LETTERS:  a e e u d k q s

WORDS TO MAKE:

Give children clues about how many letters to use and how many letters to change. "Now we're going to make some four-letter words. Add a letter to *see* and you can make *seek*." Also, give clues on what letters to change. "Change just one letter and you can change *seek* to *seed*." Alert the children when they should take all the letters out and start from scratch to make a new word. "Now take all but one letter out and make the word *ease*." For an unusual word like *ease*, give them a meaning they might understand. "The boy rode his bike with ease." Remember to give meanings for the homophones *sea* and *see* as you ask the children to make those words.

as	ask	seek	eased	quaked
	use/	seed	asked	squeak
	Sue	ease	quake	squeaked
	due	used		
	sea			
	see			

SORT FOR: s qu squ ue e (ee/ea)
ed (ending) sea-see (homophones)

WRITING AND NEED TO SPELL:
true (-ue)

blue (-ue)

(Perhaps they are writing about the colors they like!)

Copyright © 1994, Good Apple

134

G1498

LETTERS: 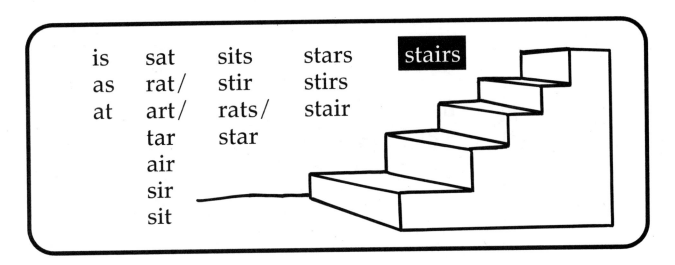 a i r s s t

WORDS TO MAKE:

Give children clues about how many letters to use and how many letters to change. "Now we're going to make some three-letter words. Add a letter to *at* and you can make *sat*." Also, give clues on what letters to change. "Change just the first letter and you can change *sat* to *rat*." For words like *rat/art/tar* which can be made from the same letters, tell the children, "Don't take any letters out. Just change the letters around and you can change *rat* into *art* then *tar*." Alert the children when they should take all the letters out and start from scratch to make a new word. "Now take all but one letter out and make the word *air*."

is	sat	sits	stars	**stairs**
as	rat/	stir	stirs	
at	art/	rats/	stair	
	tar	star		
	air			
	sir			
	sit			

SORT FOR: st   at   ir   s-pairs (sit-sits)

WRITING AND NEED TO SPELL:

> cat (-at)
>
> scat (-at)

(Perhaps they are writing about cats!)

Copyright © 1994, Good Apple

G1498

LETTERS:  a i f h r s s t

WORDS TO MAKE:

Give children clues about how many letters to use and how many letters to change. "Now we're going to make some three-letter words. Add a letter to *at* and you can make *sat*." Also, give clues on what letters to change. "Change just the first letter and you can change *sat* to *hat*." For words like *rat/tar* which can be made from the same letters, tell the children, "Don't take any letters out. Just change the letters around and you can change *rat* into *tar*." Alert the children when they should take all the letters out and start from scratch to make a new word. "Now take all but one letter out and make the four-letter word *star*."

at	sat	hair	stair	stairs	starfish
	hat	fair	stars		
	rat/	fish			
	tar	star			
	far	stir			
	air				

SORT FOR: st   ar   at   air   starfish (compound)

WRITING AND NEED TO SPELL:

chat (-at)

chair (-air)

(Perhaps they are writing about their grandmother's visit!)

Copyright © 1994, Good Apple

136

G1498

LETTERS:  i o g n p p s t

A two-day lesson or pick and choose some words.
You may want to make all words one day and sort/spell the next day.

WORDS TO MAKE:

Give children clues about how many letters to use and how many letters to change. "Now we're going to make some three-letter words. Change just the first letter and you can change *not* to *got*." For words like *tops/post/stop* which can be made from the same letters, tell the children, "Don't take any letters out. Just change the letters around and you can change *tops* into *post* then *stop*." Alert the children when they should take all the letters out and start from scratch to make a new word. "Now take all but one letter out and make the word *song*." For an unusual word like *pinto*, give the children a meaning they will understand. "The horse was called a pinto because of his color."

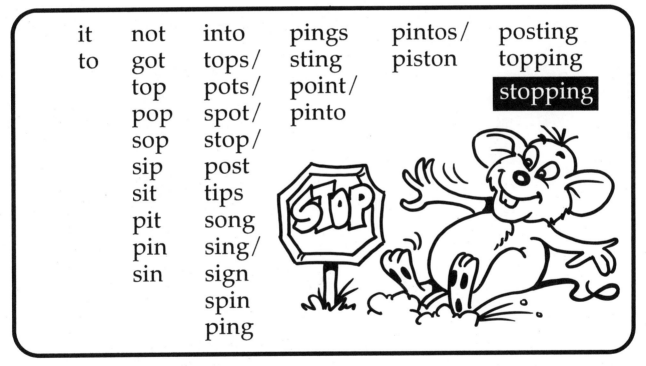

it	not	into	pings	pintos/	posting
to	got	tops/	sting	piston	topping
	top	pots/	point/		**stopping**
	pop	spot/	pinto		
	sop	stop/			
	sip	post			
	sit	tips			
	pit	song			
	pin	sing/			
	sin	sign			
		spin			
		ping			

SORT FOR: s t ot op it in ing ing (ending)

WRITING AND NEED TO SPELL:

spring (-ing)

string (-ing)

(Perhaps they are writing about flying kites!)

Copyright © 1994, Good Apple

G1498

LETTERS:  a e g n r r s t

A two-day lesson or pick and choose some words.
You may want to make all words one day and sort/spell the next day.

WORDS TO MAKE:

Give children clues about how many letters to use and how many letters to change. "Now we're going to make some three-letter words. Add a letter to *at* and you can make *art*." Give clues on what letters to change. "Change just the first letter and you can change *rat* to *sat*." For words like *eat/ate* which can be made from the same letters, tell the children, "Don't take any letters out. Just change the letters around and you can change *eat* into *ate*." Alert the children when they should take all the letters out and start from scratch to make a new word. "Now take all but one letter out and make the five-letter word *range*." Also, remind the children to turn their letters over for the capital letter they need to start the name *Stan*.)

an	art/	gate	range	strange
at	rat	rate	stare	stranger
	sat	seat	stage	
	eat/	neat		
	ate	Stan		
	ant/	star		
	tan	tear		
	ran	near		
	rag			
	tag			
	sag/			
	gas			

SORT FOR: s   t   st   at   an   ag   eat   ate

WRITING AND NEED TO SPELL:
flag (-ag)

state (-ate)

(Perhaps they are writing about the state they live in!)

Copyright © 1994, Good Apple

G1498

LETTERS: 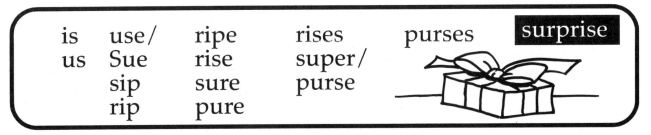 e i u p r r s s

WORDS TO MAKE:

Give children clues about how many letters to use and how many letters to change. "Now we're going to make some three-letter words. Add a letter to *us* and you can make the three letter-word *use*." Also, give clues on what letters to change. "Change just the first letter and you can change *sip* to *rip*." Alert the children when they should take all the letters out and start from scratch to make a new word. "Now take all but one letter out and make the word *rises*."

is	use/	ripe	rises	purses	**surprise**
us	Sue	rise	super/		
	sip	sure	purse		
	rip	pure			

SORT FOR: s   r   ip   s-pairs (rise-rises)

WRITING AND NEED TO SPELL: slip (-ip) slips (s)

(Perhaps they are writing about a fall on the ice!)

LETTERS:  a m p s s w

WORDS TO MAKE:

Give children clues about how many letters to use and how many letters to change. "Now we're going to make some three-letter words. Add a letter to *am* and you can make the three-letter word *Pam*." Remind the children to use the capital when making a name. They should find the capitals on the other side of their letter cards. For words like *Pam/map* which can be made from the same letters, tell the children, "Don't take any letters out. Just change the letters around and you can change *Pam* into *map*."

pa	Pam/	maps	swaps	**swamps**
ma/	map	swam	swamp	
am	paw	paws/		
	saw	swap		
	sap			

SORT FOR: sw   am   ap   aw   s (plural)

WRITING AND NEED TO SPELL: clam (-am) snap (-ap)

(Perhaps they are writing about clamming!)

Copyright © 1994, Good Apple   G1498

LETTERS:  a i g n p p t

WORDS TO MAKE:

Give children clues about how many letters to use and how many letters to change. "Now we're going to make some three-letter words. Add a letter to *in* and you can make the three-letter word *pin*." Also, give the children clues about what letters to change. "Just change the first letter in *pin* and you have the new word *tin*." For words like *tan/ant* which can be made from the same letters, tell the children, "Don't take any letters out. Just change the letters around and you can change *tan* into *ant*." For an unusual word like *pint*, give them a meaning they will understand. "There was a pint of ice cream in the freezer."

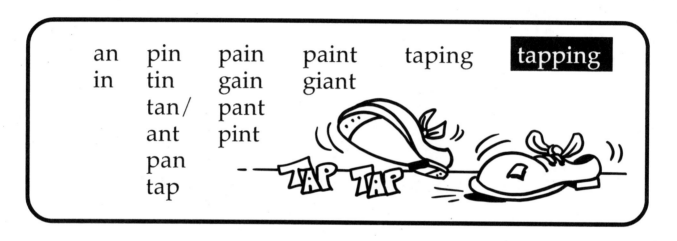

an	pin	pain	paint	taping	**tapping**
in	tin	gain	giant		
	tan/	pant			
	ant	pint			
	pan				
	tap				

SORT FOR: t p in an ain

WRITING AND NEED TO SPELL:

   win (-in)

   brain (-ain)

(Perhaps they are writing about winning on a game show!)

Copyright © 1994, Good Apple

G1498

LETTERS:  i i g h k n n t

WORDS TO MAKE:

Give children clues about how many letters to use and how many letters to change. "Now we're going to make some three-letter words. Add a letter to *in* and you can make the three-letter word *tin*." Also, give the children clues about what letters to change. "Change just the first letter in *kit* and you can make *hit*." For words like *kin/ink* which can be made from the same letters, tell the children, "Don't take any letters out. Just change the letters around and you can change *kin* into *ink*." For an unusual word like *kin*, give the children a meaning. "People in the south call their relatives their kin." Remember to also give meanings for the homophones *night* and *knight* when asking children to make those words.

it	tin	thin/	thing	knight	hinting
in	kin/	hint	think	hiking	**thinking**
	ink	knit	night		
	kit	king			
	hit				

SORT FOR: th kn in it ing ing (ending)
night-knight (homophones)

WRITING AND NEED TO SPELL:

grin (-in)

sing (-ing)

(Perhaps they are writing about a baby!)

Copyright © 1994, Good Apple

G1498

LETTERS:  o h r s t w

WORDS TO MAKE:

Give children clues about how many letters to use and how many letters to change. "Now we're going to make some four-letter words. Use four letters to make the word *stow*." Also, give the children clues about which letters to change. "Just change one letter in the word *shot* to make the new word *show*." For words like *who/how* which can be made from the same letters, tell the children, "Don't take any letters out. Just change the letters around and you can change *who* into *how*." For an unusual word like *stow*, give the children a meaning they can understand. "The man's job was to stow the goods in the truck." Remember to give meanings for the homophones *to* and *two* when asking the children to make those words.

so	two	stow	short
to	who/	shot	worth
	how	show	worst
	hot		throw
	rot		
	row		

throws

SORT FOR: sh thr ot ow to-two (homophones)

(Pull out all the *ow* words and have the children note the two common pronunciations for *o-w* in the words *how* and *show*.)

WRITING AND NEED TO SPELL:

trot (-ot)

slow (-ow)

(Perhaps they are writing about the horse that came in last in the race!)

Copyright © 1994, Good Apple

G1498

LETTERS:  e u d h n r t

WORDS TO MAKE:

Give children clues about how many letters to use and how many letters to change. "Now we're going to make some four-letter words. Add a letter to *her* and you can make the four-letter word *herd*." Alert the children when they should take all the letters out and start from scratch to make a new word. "Now take all but one letter out and make the word *turn*." Give them clues about what letters to change, "Just change one letter in *hunt* and you can make *hurt*." Remind the children to use the capital when making a name. They will find the capitals on the other side of the letter cards. For words like *Ned/den/end* which can be made from the same letters, tell the children, "Don't take any letters out. Just change the letters around and you can change *Ned* into *den* then *end*."

red	herd	under	hunted	thunder
Ted	turn		turned	
Ned/	hunt			
den/	hurt			
end				
hut				
her				

SORT FOR: t h ed u (hut/hurt) e (red/her)
ed (ending) names

WRITING AND NEED TO SPELL:

sled (-ed)

thundered (-ed)

(Perhaps they are writing about a sled race!)

Copyright © 1994, Good Apple

G1498

LETTERS:  a u d h r s t y

WORDS TO MAKE:

Give children clues about how many letters to use and how many letters to change. "Now we're going to make some three-letter words. Hold up three fingers!" Change just the first letter and you can change the word *say* into *day*." Alert the children when they should take all the letters out and start from scratch to make a new word. "Now take all the letters out and start over and make the word *shy*." Remind the children to use a capital to begin *Thursday*–the name of a day of the week. Capitals are found on the reverse side of the letter cards.

at	say	stay	dusty	sturdy	Thursday
as	day	tray	rusty		
	dry	rust	stray		
	try	dust			
	shy	duty			

SORT FOR: tr st ay ust y (try-duty)

WRITING AND NEED TO SPELL:

   clay (-ay)

   play (-ay)

(Perhaps they are writing about playing with clay!)

Copyright © 1994, Good Apple

G1498

LETTERS:  e i g r s t

WORDS TO MAKE:

Give children clues about how many letters to use and how many letters to change. "Now we're going to make some three-letter words. Hold up three fingers! Add one letter to *it* and you have *sit*. Change just the first letter and you can change the word *set* into *get*." For words like *tires/tries* which can be made from the same letters, tell the children, "Don't take any letters out. Just change the letters around and you can change *tires* into *tries*." Also, alert the children when they should take all the letters out and start from scratch to make a new word. "Now take all the letters out and start over and make the word *sir*."

is	sit	stir	tires/	tigers
it	set	tire	tries	
	get	rise	tiger	
	sir	rest		
		gets		

SORT FOR: t   et   it   ir   s pairs

WRITING AND NEED TO SPELL:

quit (-it)

quits (-s)

(Perhaps they are writing about something they have to quit doing!)

Copyright © 1994, Good Apple

G1498

LETTERS:  e e o g h r t t

WORDS TO MAKE:

Give children clues about how many letters to use and how many letters to change. "Now we're going to make some three-letter words. Hold up three fingers! Add one letter to *go* and you have *got*. Change just the first letter and you can change the word *got* into *hot*." For words like *three/there* which can be made from the same letters, tell the children, "Don't take any letters out. Just change the letters around and you can change *three* into *there*." Also, alert the children when they should take all the letters out and start from scratch to make a new word. "Now take all the letters out and start over and make the word *greet*."

to	got	tote	three/	hotter	together
go	hot	trot	there		
	the	tree	teeth		
	her		greet		
	tot		other		
			otter		

SORT FOR: t th tr ot er

(*Er* occurs in only one little word, *her*, but is a common chunk in big words. Sort for all the *er* words and help children hear its common pronunciation.)

WRITING AND NEED TO SPELL:

shot (-ot)

not (-ot)

(Perhaps they are writing about getting a shot but not crying!)

Copyright © 1994, Good Apple

G1498

LETTERS:  a c k r s t

WORDS TO MAKE:

Give children clues about how many letters to use and how many letters to change. "Now we're going to make some three-letter words. Hold up three fingers! Add one letter to *at* and you have *cat*. Change just one letter and you can change the word *rat* into *sat*." For words like *cat/act* which can be made from the same letters, tell the children, "Don't take any letters out. Just change the letters around and you can change *cat* into *act*." For an unusual word like *task*, give the children a meaning they will understand. "You must do your task before you can play."

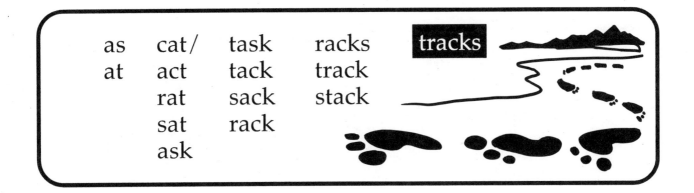

as	cat/	task	racks	tracks
at	act	tack	track	
	rat	sack	stack	
	sat	rack		
	ask			

SORT FOR: t r tr at ack ask

WRITING AND NEED TO SPELL:

black (-ack)

mask (-ask)

(Perhaps they are writing about making masks!)

Copyright © 1994, Good Apple

G1498

LETTERS:  a o c r r s t t

WORDS TO MAKE:

Give children clues about how many letters to use and how many letters to change. "Now we're going to make some three-letter words. Hold up three fingers! Add one letter to *at* and you have the three-letter word *rat*. Change just the vowel and you can change the word *rat* into *rot*." For words like *cat/act* which can be made from the same letters, tell the children, "Don't take any letters out. Just change the letters around and you can change *cat* into *act*." Also, alert the children when they should take all the letters out and start from scratch to make a new word. "Now take all the letters out and start over and make the word *roast*."

at	rat	coat	coast	carrot	tractors
	rot	cast	toast	carrots	
	cot	cost	roast	tractor	
	cat/		actor		
	act				

SORT FOR: c   r   at   oast

WRITING AND NEED TO SPELL:

hat (-at)

boast (-oast)

(Perhaps they are writing about hats they like to wear!)

Copyright © 1994, Good Apple

G1498

LETTERS:  a e e u r r s t

A two-day lesson or pick and choose some words.
You may want to make all words one day and sort/spell the next day.

WORDS TO MAKE:

Give children clues about how many letters to use and how many letters to change. "Now we're going to make some three-letter words. Add a letter to *at* and you can make the three-letter word *sat*. Change just the first letter and you can change *sat* into *rat*." For words like *rat/art* which can be made from the same letters, tell the children, "Don't take any letters out. Just change the letters around and you can change *rat* into *art*." Alert the children when they should take all the letters out and start from scratch to make a new word. "Now take all but one letter out and make the four-letter word *tree*." For an unusual word like *reuse*, give the children a meaning they will understand. "After this box is empty we will reuse it for collecting books." Remember to give meanings for the two homophones–*sea* and *see*–when asking the children to make those words.

as	sat	seat	rates	teaser	**treasure**
at	rat/	tree	reuse	rester	
	art	true	reset	eraser	
	are/	east	erase	arrest	
	ear	rear	eater		
	eat	tear/	tease		
	use	rate	trees		
	set	rats/			
	see	star			
	sea	rest			

SORT FOR: t r tr at ear er (ending)
re (prefix)   sea-see (homophones)

WRITING AND NEED TO SPELL:

that (-at)

year (-ear)

(Perhaps they are writing about an important year in their lives!)

Copyright © 1994, Good Apple

G1498

LETTERS:  e u m p r s t t

WORDS TO MAKE:

Give children clues about how many letters to use and how many letters to change. "Now we're going to make some four-letter words. Hold up four fingers! Add one letter to *pet* and you have *pets*. Change just the first letter and you can change the word *pest* into *test*." For words like *pets/pest* which can be made from the same letters, tell the children, "Don't take any letters out. Just change the letters around and you can change *pets* into *pest*." Also, alert the children when they should take all the letters out and start from scratch to make a new word. "Now take all the letters out and start over and make the word *must*." For an unusual word like *trump*, give the children a meaning they will understand. "In some card games, one of the suits is the trump suit."

me	met	pets/	trust	trumpet	**trumpets**
	set	pest	trump		
	pet	test	stump		
		rest			
		rump			
		must			
		rust			

SORT FOR: m r t tr et est ust ump

WRITING AND NEED TO SPELL:

best (-est)

jump (-ump)

(Perhaps they are writing about a jumping contest!)

Copyright © 1994, Good Apple

G1498

LETTERS:  i u n p r s t

WORDS TO MAKE:

Give children clues about how many letters to use and how many letters to change. "Now we're going to make some three-letter words. Hold up three fingers! Add one letter to *it* and you have *pit*. Change just the first letter and you can change the word *pit* into *sit*." For words like *stun/nuts* which can be made from the same letters, tell the children, "Don't take any letters out. Just change the letters around and you can change *stun* into *nuts*." Also, alert the children when they should take all the letters out and start from scratch to make a new word. "Now take all the letters out and start over and make the word *spin*." For an unusual word like *spur*, give the children a meaning they will understand. "The cowboy urged the horse on with his spur."

it	pit	stun/	spurt	sprint	turnips
	sit	nuts	print	turnip	
	run	spin			
	sun	spit			
		suit			
		spur			

SORT FOR: sp un it

WRITING AND NEED TO SPELL:

run (-un)

spit (-it)

(Perhaps they are writing about an angry cat!)

LETTERS:  e i u k n p r t

WORDS TO MAKE:

Give children clues about how many letters to use and how many letters to change. "Now we're going to make some three-letter words. Hold up three fingers! Add one letter to *in* and you have *ink*. Change just one letter and you can change the word *tip* into *rip*." Alert the children when they should take all the letters out and start from scratch to make a new word. "Now take all the letters out and start over and make the word *kite*." For an unusual word like *punk*, give the children a meaning they will understand. "The rock singer liked to dress like a punk."

it	ink	pink	untie	turnip	turnpike
in	tip	punk	trunk	unripe	
	rip	kite			
	pie	trip			
		true			

SORT FOR: tr ip unk un (prefix)

WRITING AND NEED TO SPELL:

    dunk (-unk)

    sip (-ip)

(Perhaps they are writing about eating donuts!)

Copyright © 1994, Good Apple

G1498

LETTERS:  e u l r s t t

WORDS TO MAKE:

Give children clues about how many letters to use and how many letters to change. "Now we're going to make some four-letter words. Hold up four fingers! Change just the vowel and you can change the word *rust* into *rest*." Alert the children when they should take all the letters out and start from scratch to make a new word. "Now take all the letters out and start over and make the word *true*." For an unusual word like *strut*, give the children a meaning they will understand. "The boys strut down the hall as the children watch them."

let	rust	rules	result/	turtles
set	rest	trust/	rustle	
rut	test	strut	turtle	
	true			
	user			
	rule			

SORT FOR: t tr est ut ust le (turtle)

WRITING AND NEED TO SPELL:

best (-est)

dust (-ust)

(Perhaps they are writing about cleaning up their rooms!)

Copyright © 1994, Good Apple

LETTERS:  e i k l n t w

WORDS TO MAKE:

Give children clues about how many letters to use and how many letters to change. "Now we're going to make some three-letter words. Hold up three fingers! Add one letter to *it* and you have *kit*. Change just the first letter and you can change the word *kit* into *wit*." For words like *net/ten* which can be made from the same letters, tell the children, "Don't take any letters out. Just change the letters around and you can change *net* into *ten*." Also, alert the children when they should take all the letters out and start from scratch to make a new word. "Now take all the letters out and start over and make the word *tin*." For an unusual word like *link*, give the children a meaning they will understand. "The teacher told the class to link their hands together to make a big circle." Remember to give the meanings for the homophones *new* and *knew* as you ask the children to make them.

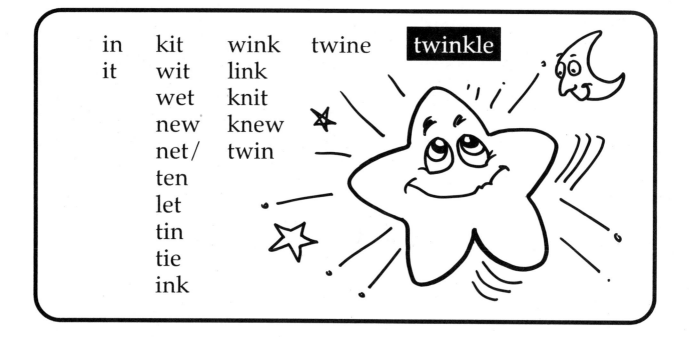

in	kit	wink	twine	twinkle
it	wit	link		
	wet	knit		
	new	knew		
	net/	twin		
	ten			
	let			
	tin			
	tie			
	ink			

SORT FOR: t   w   tw   kn   in   it   ink   et
new-knew (homophones)

WRITING AND NEED TO SPELL:

quit (-it)

rink (-ink)

(Perhaps they are writing about roller skating!)

Copyright © 1994, Good Apple

G1498

LETTERS:  a e l l s v y

WORDS TO MAKE:

Give children clues about how many letters to use and how many letters to change. "Now we're going to make some four-letter words. Hold up four fingers! Change just the first letter and you can change the word *yell* into *sell*." For words like *seal/sale* which can be made from the same letters, tell the children, "Don't take any letters out. Just change the letters around and you can change *seal* into *sale*." Also, alert the children when they should take all the letters out and start from scratch to make a new word. "Now take all the letters out and start over and make the word *slay*." For an unusual word like *alley*, give the children a meaning they will understand. "The alley was located between some buildings on the main street."

as	say	yell	yells	valley	**valleys**
	lay	sell	alley		
	yes	seal/	slave		
		sale			
		save/			
		vase			
		slay			

SORT FOR: v   y   s   ay   ell

WRITING AND NEED TO SPELL:

hay (-ay)

smell (-ell)

(Perhaps they are writing about being on the farm!)

Copyright © 1994, Good Apple

G1498

LETTERS:  e e i c h l v

WORDS TO MAKE:

Give children clues about how many letters to use and how many letters to change. "Now we're going to make some four-letter words. Hold up four fingers! Add one letter to *ice* and you have the four-letter word *vice*. Change just one letter and you can change the word *vice* into *lice*." For words like *live/evil/vile* which can be made from the same letters, tell the children, "Don't take any letters out. Just change the letters around and you can change *live* into *evil* then *vile*." Also, alert the children when they should take all the letters out and start from scratch to make a new word. "Now take all the letters out and start over and make the word *heel*." For an unusual word like *vile*, give the children a meaning they will understand. "The man got angry and used mean, nasty, vile language."

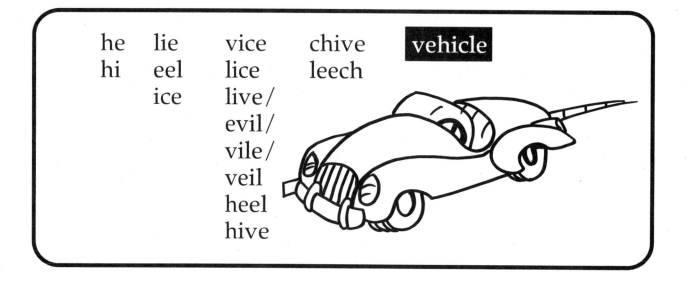

he	lie	vice	chive	**vehicle**
hi	eel	lice	leech	
	ice	live/		
		evil/		
		vile/		
		veil		
		heel		
		hive		

SORT FOR: v   h   l   ice   ive

WRITING AND NEED TO SPELL:

twice (-ice)

drive (-ive)

(Perhaps they are writing about bumper cars at an amusement park!)

Copyright © 1994, Good Apple

G1498

LETTERS:  a e i g l l v

WORDS TO MAKE:

Give children clues about how many letters to use and how many letters to change. "Now we're going to make some four-letter words. Hold up four fingers! Add one letter to *lie* and you have the four-letter word *live*. Change just one letter and you can change the word *live* into *give*." For words like *evil/veil* which can be made from the same letters, tell the children, "Don't take any letters out. Just change the letters around and you can change *evil* into *veil*." Also, alert the children when they should take all the letters out and start over and make the word *agile*." For an unusual word like *agile*, give the children a meaning they will understand. "The secretary had agile fingers and typed very fast." Remember to give the children a meaning for the homophones *veil* and *vale* when asking them to spell those words.

Al	all	live	agile	village
	ill	give	alive	
	age	gave		
	lag	evil/		
	leg	veil		
	lie	vale/		
		veal		

SORT FOR: v l ive vale-veil (homophones)
(Point out the two pronunciations for *live*.)

WRITING AND NEED TO SPELL:

hive (-ive)

five (-ive)

(Perhaps they are writing about a beekeeper or insects!)

Copyright © 1994, Good Apple

G1498

LETTERS:  a i g k l n w

WORDS TO MAKE:

Give children clues about how many letters to use and how many letters to change. "Now we're going to make some three-letter words. Hold up three fingers! Add one letter to *in* and you have *ink*. Change just one letter and you can change the word *kin* into *win*." For words like *ink/kin* which can be made from the same letters, tell the children, "Don't take any letters out. Just change the letters around and you can change *ink* into *kin*." Also, alert the children when they should take all the letters out and start from scratch to make a new word. "Now take all the letters out and start over and make the word *waking*."

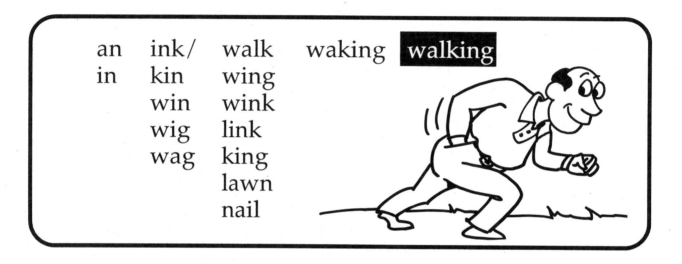

an	ink/	walk	waking	walking
in	kin	wing		
	win	wink		
	wig	link		
	wag	king		
		lawn		
		nail		

SORT FOR: w   in   ink   ing

WRITING AND NEED TO SPELL:
   drink (-ink)
   shrink (-ink)

(Perhaps they are writing about a magic potion!)

LETTERS:  e i h k r s s w

WORDS TO MAKE:

Give children clues about how many letters to use and how many letters to change. "Now we're going to make some four-letter words. Hold up four fingers! Change just the first letter and you can change the word *wire* into *hire*." Alert the children when they should take all the letters out and start from scratch to make a new word. "Now take all the letters out and start over and make the word *kiss*." For an unusual word like *whisk*, give the children a meaning they will understand. "They will whisk the winner off the stage so people will not crowd her."

we	his	wire	skier	kisser	whisker
he	she	hire	hiker		whiskers
is	ski	hike	whisk		
		kiss			
		wish			

SORT FOR: w h wh e (he) ire er (ending)

(Help the children to see that sometimes *er* is an ending as in *skier*, *kisser*, and *hiker*, and sometimes *er* is just the last chunk in a word as in *whisker*.)

WRITING AND NEED TO SPELL:

she (-e)

fire (-ire)

(Perhaps they are writing about a fire or camping!)

Copyright © 1994, Good Apple

LETTERS:  i o d n s w w

WORDS TO MAKE:

Give children clues about how many letters to use and how many letters to change. "Now we're going to make some three-letter words. Hold up three fingers! Add one letter to *in* and you have *sin*. Change just the vowel and you can change the word *sin* into *son*." For an unusual word like *widow*, give the children a meaning they will understand. "The man was killed in an accident, leaving his wife a widow with three children."

is	sin	wins	winds	widows	windows
in	son	wind	widow	window	
	sod				
	nod				
	now				
	sow				
	wow				
	win				

SORT FOR: w in od ow

(Point out the two common sounds for *ow* as in *now* and *window* and the two pronunciations for *sow*.)

WRITING AND NEED TO SPELL:

rod (-od)

how (-ow)

(Perhaps they are writing about teaching someone how to fish!)

Copyright © 1994, Good Apple

G1498

LETTERS:  e i n r t w

WORDS TO MAKE:

Give children clues about how many letters to use and how many letters to change. "Now we're going to make some three-letter words. Hold up three fingers! Add one letter to *in* and you have *win*. Change just the first letter and you can change the word *win* into *tin*." For words like *ten/net* which can be made from the same letters, tell the children, "Don't take any letters out. Just change the letters around and you can change *ten* into *net*." Also, alert the children when they should take all the letters out and start from scratch to make a new word. "Now take all the letters out and start over and make the word *twin*." For an unusual word like *wren*, give the children a meaning they will understand. "Outside my window the wren sat in the tree and sang a song."

in	win	tire	twine	**winter**
	tin	twin	write	
	ten/	wire		
	net	went		
	tie	wren		
		wine		

SORT FOR: t   w   tw   wr   in   ine   ire

WRITING AND NEED TO SPELL:
skin (-in)
spine (-ine)
(Perhaps they are writing about a checkup at the doctor's!)

Copyright © 1994, Good Apple

G1498

LETTERS:  *e i c h s t w*

WORDS TO MAKE:

Give children clues about how many letters to use and how many letters to change. "Now we're going to make some four-letter words. Hold up four fingers! Add one letter to *his* and you have *hits*. Change just one letter and you can change the word *wish* into *with*." For words like *its/sit* which can be made from the same letters, tell the children, "Don't take any letters out. Just change the letters around and you can change *its* into *sit*."

is	its/	hits	white	switch	witches
it	sit	itch	witch	itches	
	hit	wish			
	his	with			

SORT FOR: w   it   s/es (plural)

WRITING AND NEED TO SPELL:

kits (-it, -s)

wishes (-es plural)

(Perhaps they are writing about things on their wish list!)

Copyright © 1994, Good Apple

G1498

LETTERS:  iogknrw

WORDS TO MAKE:

Give children clues about how many letters to use and how many letters to change. "Now we're going to make some three-letter words. Hold up three fingers! Add one letter to *in* and you have *win*. Change just the first letter and you can change the four-letter word *wink* into *rink*." For words like *kin/ink* which can be made from the same letters, tell the children, "Don't take any letters out. Just change the letters around and you can change *kin* into *ink*." Also, alert the children when they should take all the letters out and start from scratch to make a new word. "Now take all the letters out and start over and make the word *wrong*." For the homophones *ring* and *wring*, give the children meanings as you ask them to make these words.

in	win	wink	wrong	rowing
kin/	rink	wring	working
ink	ring		
row	king		
	wing		
	work		
	worn		

SORT FOR: w   wr   in   ink   ing   ing (ending)
ring-wring (homophones)

WRITING AND NEED TO SPELL:
think (-ink)

singing (-ing)

(Perhaps they are writing about school!)

Copyright © 1994, Good Apple

G1498

LETTERS:  e o u f l r s y

A two-day lesson or pick and choose some words.
You may want to make all the words one day and sort/spell the next day.

WORDS TO MAKE:

Give children clues about how many letters to use and how many letters to change. "Now we're going to make some four-letter words. Hold up four fingers! Add one letter to *our* and you have *your*. Change just the first letter and you can change the word *your* into *four*." Alert the children when they should take all the letters out and start from scratch to make a new word. "Now take all the letters out and start over and make the word *fury*." For an unusual word like *surely*, give the children a meaning they will understand. "The girl will surely win the race."

of	use	your	lousy	sorely	ourself
us	you	four	rules	surely	**yourself**
	yes	sour			
	sly	sure			
	fly	sore			
	elf	self			
	for	fore			
	our	fury			
		user			
		rule			
		rely			
		rose			
		rosy			

SORT FOR: y (you, sly, rosy) elf our
ly (ending) for-four (homophones)

(Point out the two common pronunciations for *our* as in *our-your*.)

WRITING AND NEED TO SPELL:
shelf (-elf)

flour (-our)

(Perhaps they are writing about grocery shopping!)

Copyright © 1994, Good Apple

G1498

LETTERS: a e b r s z

WORDS TO MAKE:

Give children clues about how many letters to use and how many letters to change. "Add one letter to *ears* and you have *bears*." For words like *ear/are* which can be made from the same letters, tell the children, "Don't take any letters out. Just change the letters around and you can change *ear* into *are*."

be	sea	bars	bears	zebras
as	ear	bare	zebra	
	are	base		
	bar	bear		
		ears		

SORT FOR: b ear s (plural) s (pairs)

WRITING AND NEED TO SPELL: bases (-s) near (-ear)

(Perhaps they are writing about playing baseball!)

LETTERS: e i p p r s z

WORDS TO MAKE:

Give children clues about how many letters to use and how many letters to change. "Now we're going to make some four-letter words. Hold up four fingers! Change just the first letter and you can change the word *pipe* into *ripe*." For words like *ripe/pier* which can be made from the same letters, tell the children, "Don't take any letters out. Just change the letters around and you can change *ripe* into *pier*." Also, alert the children when they should take all the letters out and start from scratch to make a new word. "Now take all the letters out and start over and make the word *size*." Give meanings for the homophones *prize* and *pries*. "She pries open the lid of the jar."

is	sip	pipe	prize	prizes
	zip	ripe/	pries	zipper
	rip	pier	pipes	zippers
	sir	pies		
	pie	size		

SORT FOR: z p pr ip ipe ize s-pairs
prize-pries (homophones)

WRITING AND NEED TO SPELL: drip (-ip) stripe (-ipe)

(Perhaps they are writing about painting pictures!)

Copyright © 1994, Good Apple

G1498

MAKING WORDS
Index of Patterns

Prefixes/Suffixes/Endings

ed	counted, doorbell, laughed, scared, searched, squeaked, thunder
en (eaten)	golden, princess
er (painter)	breaking, drivers, earrings, reindeer, together, treasure, whiskers
er/est	pictures
ing	breaking, duckling, sleeping, stopping, thinking, working
le	turtles
ly	yourself
re	creature, earrings, present, treasure
s/es	apples, baseball, baskets, beaches, biggest, bridges, candles, chickens, chairs, clouds, covers, cowboys, dances, engines, farmers, fishing, glasses, globes, kitchens, kittens, lizards, millions, monkeys, muffins, oranges, peanuts, pebbles, potatoes, princess, puppies, quarters, roosters, seashells, searched, sniffing, splash, squeaked, stairs, surprises, swamps, witches, zebras
un	turnpike
y (rainy)	Saturday, Thursday, yourself

Consonants/Blends/Digraphs

b	balloons, baseball, baskets, bathtubs, beaches, biggest, blanket, breaking, bridges, cowboys, keyboard, pebbles, sailboat, thumbs, zebras
bl	blanket, sailboat
br	breaking, bridges, keyboard
c (cat/city)	beaches, camera, candles, cassette, castle, cereals, chairs, chapter, clouds, computer, cookies, counted, country, covers, cowboys, crackers, creature, dances, scared, scratch, searched, tractors
ch	chairs, chapter, cheering, chickens, searched
cl	candles, clouds, duckling
cr	camera, crackers, creature
d	addition, dances, darling, daughter, dinner, doctor, dreams, drivers, duckling, keyboard, picked, reindeer
dr	darling, daughter, dragon, dreams, drivers
f	farmers, feathers, fishing, flowers, forehead, friends, goldfish, yourself
fl	flowers
fr	farmers, friends
g (girl/gym)	giants, glasses, globes, golden, goldfish, quacking
gl	glasses, globes, laughed
gr	darling, morning, parking
h	anywhere, bathtubs, chairs, chapter, cheering, chickens, feathers, forehead, helping, hunting, nights, sandwich, searched, thunder, vehicles, whiskers
j	jumping, jungles
k	keyboard, kitchens, kittens

Copyright © 1994, Good Apple

G1498

kn	thinking, twinkle
l	always, balloons, blanket, candles, duckling, flowers, glasses, globes, golden, helping, laughed, lights, lizards, playpen, vehicles, village
m	Amelia, magnets, millions, monkeys, monster, morning, mothers, mountain, muffins, oatmeal, problem, smallest, trumpets
n	counted, magnets, monster, peanuts
p	apples, asleep, elephant, helping, jumping, palace, panther, parades, parents, parking, parrots, peanuts, pebbles, picked, pictures, planets, playpen, pockets, potatoes, present, princess, pumpkins, puppies, sleeping, spring, tapping, spider, spring, zipper
pl	elephant, planets, playpen
pr	princess, problems, parrots, zippers
qu	quacking, quarters, squeaked
r	bridges, camera, covers, crackers, creature, daughter, dinner, doorbell, drivers, earrings, farmers, forehead, morning, oranges, parking, parrots, princess, problems, quarter, rabbits, raking, reindeer, roosters, spring, surprise, tracks, tractors, treasure, trumpets, trunks
s	always, animals, asleep, baseball, baskets, cassette, castle, cereals, dances, earrings, engines, giants, glasses, island, kitchens, kittens, lights, millions, monkeys, nights, pockets, sailboat, sandwich, Saturday, scared, seashell, sleeping, smallest, sniffing, spider, splash, squeaked, stopping, stranger, strong, surprise, tricks, valleys, yourself
sc	cereals, scared, scratch
sh	pushed, seashell, shadow, throws, pushed
sk	kitchens, kittens, tricks, pumpkins
sl	always, animals, lights, sleeping, splash, sailboat
sm	monkeys, smallest
sn	muffins, sniffing
sp	pockets, pumpkins, pushed, spends, spider, sports, turnips
squ	quarters, squeaked
st	giants, pockets, potatoes, rabbits, Saturday, stairs, starfish, strange, strength, Thursday, tricks, trunks
sw	swamps
t	bathtubs, country, giants, hunting, monster, mothers, mountain, oatmeal, peanuts, potatoes, roosters, stranger, stopping, strong, tapping, thunder, tiger, together, topping, tracks, treasure, turtles, twinkle, winter
th	bathtubs, hunting, thinking, together
thr	throws
tr	Saturday, Thursday, tracks, treasure, trumpets, turnpike, turtles
tw	twinkle, winter
v	valleys, vehicles, village
w	anywhere, twinkle, walking, whiskers, windows, winter, witches, working
wh	anywhere, whiskers
wr	winter, working
y	keyboard, valleys, yourself
z	zippers

Copyright © 1994, Good Apple

G1498

Phonograms/Rhymes/Chunks

ab	balloons, bathtubs, sailboat
ace	camera, cereals, palace
ack*	crackers, tracks
ad	addition, dances, forehead, island, laughed, lizards, parades, sandwich, searched, shadow
ag	breaking, giants, glasses, oranges, stranger
age	oranges
ail	Amelia, animals, island, lizards, sailboat
ain*	animals, darling, earrings, giants, parking, raking, tapping
air	chairs, starfish
ake*	baskets, blanket, breaking, crackers, keyboard
al	animals, splash
ale*	asleep, baseball, castle, cereal, oatmeal
all*	smallest
am	animals, camera, dreams, farmers, swamp
ame*	farmers
an*	addition, blanket, candles, dances, darling, elephant, magnets, mountain, peanuts, planets, playpen, stranger, tapping
and	candles, dances, darling, island, sandwich
ank*	blanket
ant	patents
ap*	apples, palace, parades, playpen, splash, swamps
ar	parades, rabbits, scared, scratch, starfish
are	scared, crackers
art	chapter, daughter, scratch
ash*	beaches, chairs, scratch, shadow, splash
ask	tracks
ass	glasses
ast	castle
aste	potatoes
at*	baskets, bathtubs, cassette, castle, chapter, creature, daughter, feathers, magnets, panther, parents, parrots, peanuts, planets, potatoes, quarters, rabbits, sailboat, scratch, Saturday, smallest, stairs, starfish, stranger, stairs, tracks, tractors, treasure
ate*	cassette, creature, planets, stranger
aw*	always, swamps
ay*	always, keyboard, playpen, Saturday, skylab, Thursday, valleys
e (he)	whiskers
each	chapter
eal	asleep, oatmeal
ear (hear/pear)	anywhere, creature, dreams, earrings, farmers, forehead, scared, searched, zebras
ease	cassette, cereals
eat*	blanket, cassette, castle, chapter, feathers, magnets, oatmeal, panther, peanuts, stranger
eck	chickens, picked
ed	bridges, dinner, doorbell, forehead, keyboard, pushed, spends, thunder

Copyright © 1994, Good Apple

G1498

ee	asleep, pebbles
eed	reindeer
eel	pebbles
eep	pebbles, sleeping
eet	feathers
eg	helping
elf	yourself
ell*	baseball, seashell, smallest, valleys
en	blanket, elephant, helping, magnets, monster, spends, strength
end	spend
ent	parents, present
er	together
est*	peanuts, present, quarters, strength, trumpets
et	biggest, blanket, panther, parents, peanuts, pictures, planets, present, smallest, strength, tigers, trumpets, twinkle
ice*	cheering, picked, pictures, princess, vehicle
ick*	chickens, duckling, quacking, tricks
id	duckling
ide*	drivers, bridges, spider
idge	bridges
ie (tie)	helping, picked, pictures
ig	bridges, jumping
ight*	lights, nights
ill*	millions
im	morning
in*	cheering, engines, fishing, friends, hunting, island, kitchen, kittens, morning, muffins, parking, princess, pumpkins, raking, sleeping, spring, stopping, tapping, thinking, twinkle, walking, windows, working
ine	dinner, helping, princess, winter
ing*	nights, raking, sleeping, spring, stopping, thinking, walking, working
inge	cheering
ink*	kitchen, parking, pumpkins, twinkle, walking, working
ip*	helping, parking, surprise, spider, turnpike
ir	friends, tigers
ire	whiskers
ish	sandwich
it*	biggest, kitchen, kittens, lights, nights, pictures, sailboat, stopping, thinking, tricks, turnips, twinkle, witches
ive	drivers, vehicles, village
ize	zippers
oast	tractors
ob	globes, problems
ock*	pockets
od	clouds, doctor, windows
og	golden
oil	goldfish, sailboat

Copyright © 1994, Good Apple

G1498

oke*	monkeys
old	clouds, golden, goldfish
ole	problems
one	monster
ong	strong
oo	cowboys
oon	balloons
op*	computer, parrots, pockets, problems, stopping
ore*	computer, covers, mothers, roosters, wrote
orn	country
ot*	computer, counted, doctor, monster, parrots, pockets, potatoes, sailboat, sports, stopping, strong, together, throws
our (our/four)	yourself
ove	covers
ow (how/show)	cowboys, flowers, windows, throws
oy	country, cowboys, keyboard
ub	bathtubs, thumbs
uck*	duckling
ue	pushed, squeaked
uff	muffins
ug*	daughter, hunting, jumping, jungles, laughed
ump*	trumpets
un	jumping, jungles, muffins, trunks, turnips
ung	jungles
unk*	pumpkins, turnpike
up	puppies
ust	Saturday, Thursday, trumpets, turtles
ut	counted, country, thumbs, trunks, turtles
y (fly/fishy)	Saturday, skylab, Thursday, yourself

(*indicates one of the most common phonograms)

Copyright © 1994, Good Apple

G1498

Homophones

ad-add	addition
bear-bare	breaking
boar-bore	keyboard
board-bored	keyboard
brake-break	breaking, keyboard
dear-deer	forehead
feat-feet	feathers
for-four	yourself
heal-heel	seashell
hear-here	anywhere, searched
in-inn	dinner, engines, sniffing
mail-male	Amelia
new-knew	twinkle
night-knight	thinking
or-ore	covers, mothers
or-ore-oar	keyboard
peal-peel	asleep, elephant
pear-pare	parades
prize-pries	zippers
rein-rain-reign	earrings
read-reed	forehead
red-read	keyboard
real-reel	cereal
ring-wring	working
road-rode	keyboard
roll-role	doorbell
rose-rows	flowers
sea-see	asleep, beaches, cereals, seashell, squeaked, treasure
to-too	doctor
to-two	throws
vale-veil	village
wear-where	anywhere

Compound Words

anywhere	anywhere
baseball	baseball
bathtubs	bathtubs
bedroll	doorbell
cowboys	cowboys
doorbell	doorbell
goldfish	goldfish
into	addition, mountain
keyboard	keyboard
oatmeal	oatmeal
playpen	playpen
sailboat	sailboat
seashell	seashell
starfish	starfish
teapot	potatoes
upset	peanuts
yourself	yourself

Copyright © 1994, Good Apple

G1498

Dear Family,

Making Words is an important activity we work on in our class. Making Words is an active, hands-on activity that children learn by doing. Each day as we "make words" your child learns more about letters and letter sounds (phonics). As children manipulate the letters they are given, they have an opportunity to discover more about letter-sound relationships, and as they look for patterns in words, they have an opportunity to see how these letter-sound relationships work in words. These two activities help children both to read and spell even more words! The children enjoy these lessons, but more importantly, these skills increase their word knowledge.

Please work with the letters your child will be bringing home. Let them cut the letter strips apart into the individual letters. Then work together and see how many words you can make. As you make the words write them in the blanks. Finally, cut the words apart and group them (your child knows what to do). Have fun working together and good luck!

Sincerely,

Your child's teacher

Take-Home Sheet for Making Words

The letters you need to "Make Words" tonight are at the top of the page. First, cut the letters apart; then work together to see how many words you can make. Next, let your child write the words in the blanks. Finally, cut the words apart and sort or group them by beginning (ending) sounds or spelling patterns.

Copyright © 1994. Good Apple

G1498

The letters need to be printed lowercase on one side and uppercase on the other so the two pages can be run back to back. You need two of every vowel. The teacher reproduces a page for each child in his or her class on (red index card) paper.

a	a	a	a
e	e	e	e
i	i	i	o
o	o	u	u
u	y	y	y

Copyright © 1994. Good Apple

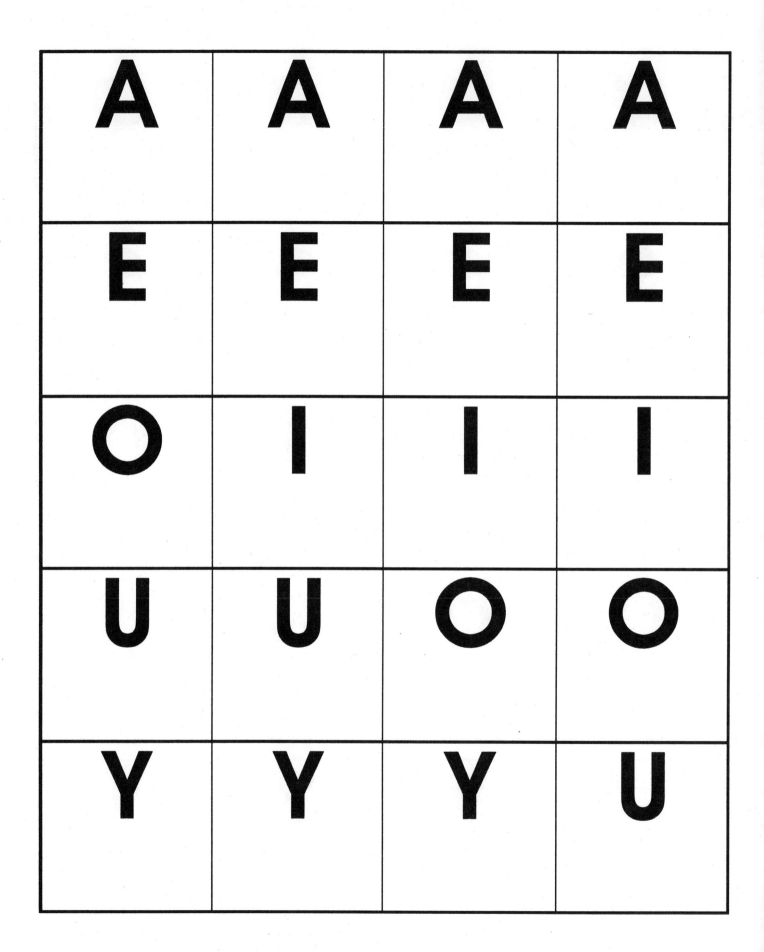

Copyright © 1994, Good Apple

G1498

The teacher reproduces the consonant pages (on white index card) for each child in his or her class. You need two of *most* consonants.

b	b	c	c
d	d	f	f
g	g	h	h
j	j	k	k
l	l	m	m

Copyright © 1994, Good Apple

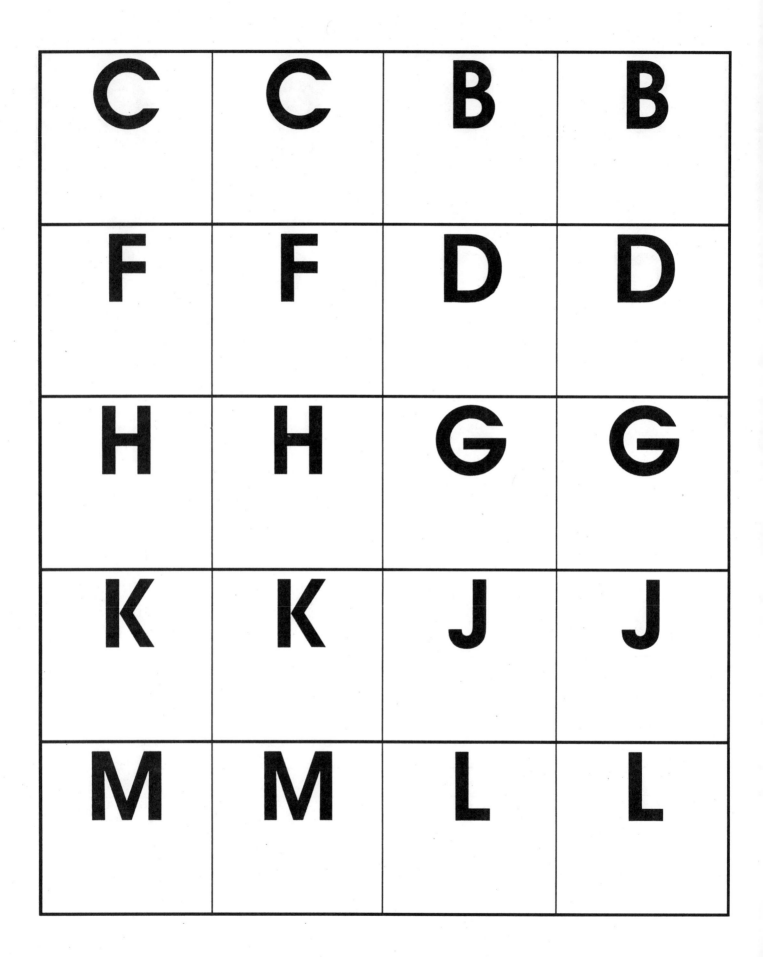

Copyright © 1994, Good Apple

n	n	p	p
q	q	r	r
s	s	t	t
v	v	w	w
x	x	z	z

Copyright © 1994. Good Apple

G1498

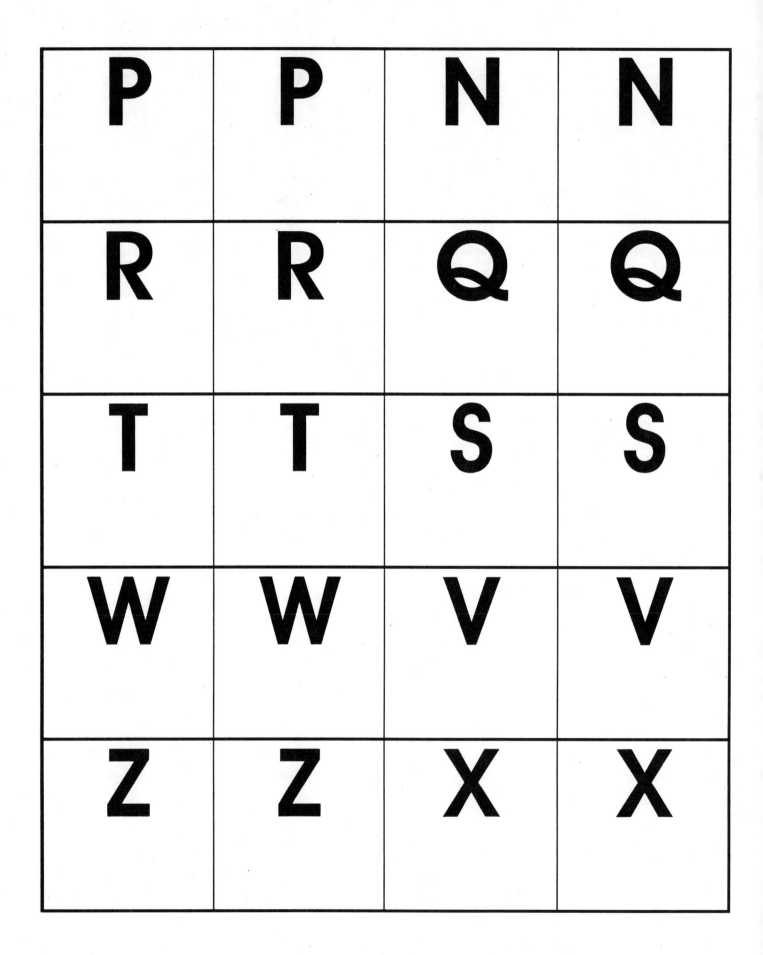

Copyright © 1994, Good Apple

G1498